AF513298

Collins

Science Expert 3

Authors

Meenakshi Atal

Debahuti Das

Components of DigiSuite

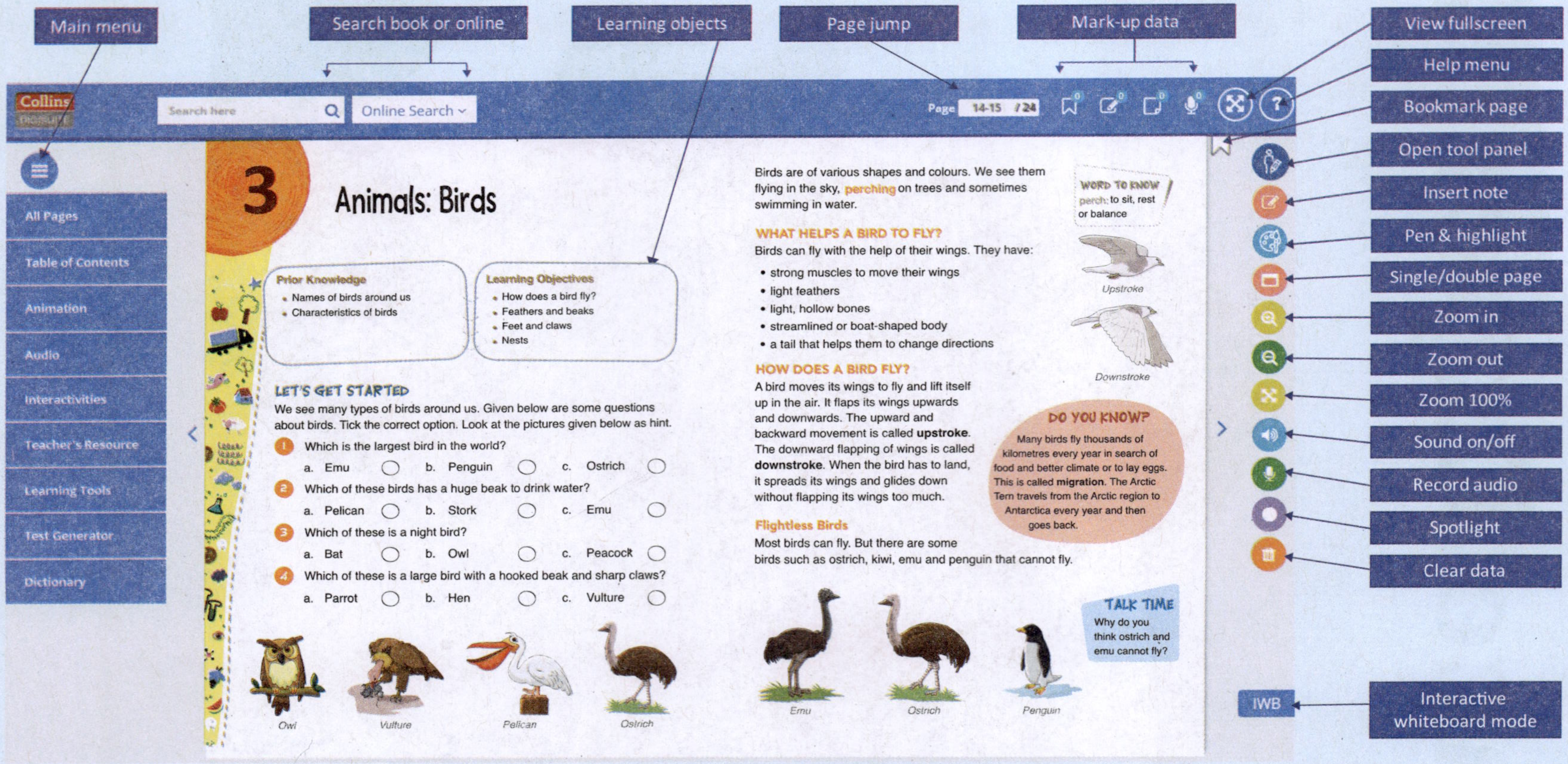

Student + Teacher			Teacher-only	
a animations	**ia** activities	**g** games	**lp** lesson plans	**tn** teacher's notes
ilt instructor-led tutorials	**w** worksheets	**v** videos	**w** worksheets	**ak** answer keys
	audio			

Preface

Collins Science Expert is a series of 14 coursebooks for Classes 1 to 8. The coursebooks for grades 1 and 2 are aligned with Environmental Studies (EVS) and grades 3 to 5 with Science. For Classes 6 to 8, there are separate coursebooks for Physics, Chemistry and Biology. This series, which is the revised edition of *Science Panorama*, is based on the **latest curriculum** prescribed by the **Council for the Indian School Certificate Examinations** and adheres to the guidelines of the *National Education Policy* (NEP) 2020.

In line with the curriculum, a thematic, coherent and structured approach has been followed and all new topics suggested in the curriculum have been included. The series also caters to the three domains of learning—**cognitive** (*intellectual nature*), **affective** (*attitudinal nature*) and **psychomotor** (*actionable nature*).

Aimed to answer a learner's cry: '*Teach me the way I want to learn*', this series adopts a method—**visual**, **auditory**, **kinesthetic** and **tactile** (**VAKT**)—that caters to all kinds of learners. Keeping in mind the saying 'I hear – I forget, I see – I understand and I do – I remember', a lot of hands-on activities have been incorporated. This would enable learners to understand and learn scientific concepts through experiential learning.

This series also emphasizes on developing *scientific skills* such as **observation**, **data collection**, **investigation**, **estimation**, **prediction**, **analysis** and **drawing inferences**. This would help in developing a scientific temperament in learners from a young age. The series also draws a connection between cause and effect; and focuses on the application of concepts in real-life situations. The language used is child-friendly and age-appropriate. Sufficient examples from everyday life have been given to help learners understand the concepts. A lot of colourful illustrations and well-labelled diagrams have been included to engage learners and aid in their understanding.

We would like to take this opportunity to thank all the teachers who reviewed the books and provided their valuable feedback, which helped in improving the quality of the content.

Any suggestions or constructive criticism from the users are welcome. We shall try to incorporate those in the future editions.

Authors

Key Features

The key features of ***Collins Science Expert*** series are completely aligned with *National Education Policy* (NEP) 2020. These meticulously designed key features, based on VAKT (visual, auditory, kinesthetic and tactile) learning style and the three domains of Bloom's Taxonomy which include **cognitive (intellectual skills)**, **affective (attitudinal nature)** and **psychomotor (actionable nature)**, can be used as learning strategies to help in the development of scientific and 21st Century Skills in students. These key features also aim to help students shift from rote-learning to competency-based learning.

Bloom's Taxonomy

Cognitive Domain

- Focuses on intellectual skills such as critical thinking, problem solving, and creating a knowledge base
- Expects learners to progress linearly, beginning at "remember" and ending at "create."

Features:
- Prior Knowledge
- Learning Objectives
- Let's Get Started
- Quick Revision
- Talk Time
- Concept Map
- Keywords
- Exercise
- Word to know
- Review Corner

Affective Domain

- Focuses on the attitudes, values, interests and appreciation of learners
- Focuses on allowing learners to understand what their own values are and how they have developed

Features:
- Greenathon
- Skill Booster
- Worksheets
- My Environment, My Responsibility!
- Happy Accidents
- Innovation: The Steppingstone
- Role of Science in Benefitting the Society

Psycho motor Domain

- Encompasses the ability of learners to physically accomplish tasks and perform movement and skills
- Expects learners to progress from using reflexes and basic movement to non-discursive communication and meaningfully expressive activity

Features:
- Do It Yourself
- Activities
- Skill Booster
- Worksheets
- My Eco Craft
- Innovation: The Steppingstone
- STEAM Worksheets

Skills and Learnings

Colour-coded tags and icons are used to easily identify the types of skills and learnings being addressed.

NEP Aligned Skills

21st Century Skills (21CS)

Learning Skills
- Critical Thinking
- Creativity and Innovation
- Collaboration
- Communication

Life Skills
- Flexibility and Adaptability
- Leadership and Responsibility
- Initiative and Self-direction
- Productivity and Accountability
- Social and Cross-cultural Interaction

Literacy Skills
- Information Literacy
- Media Literacy
- Technology Literacy

Experiential Learning (EL)

Cross Curricular (CC)

Bloom's Taxonomy (BT)

Art Integration (AI)

India Focus (IF)

SEE Learning

About the Features

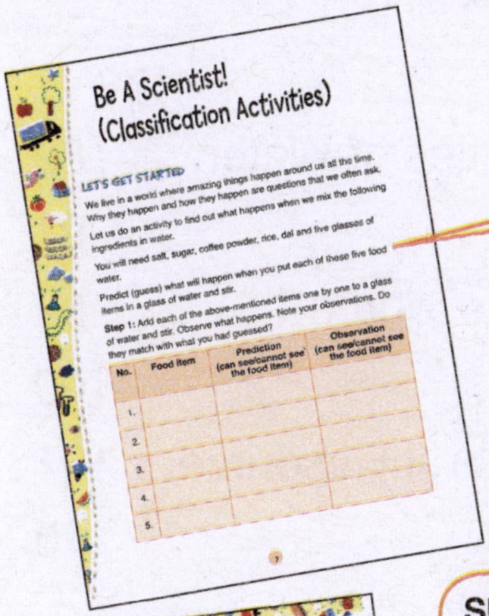

Be a Scientist! (Classes 3 to 5): Introduction to science process skills to help develop scientific attitudes

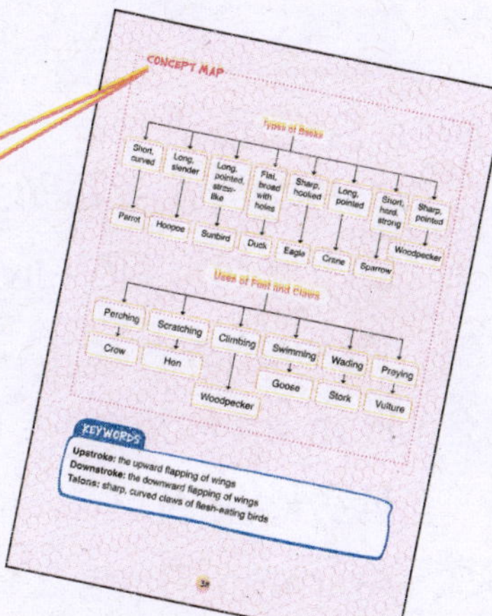

- **Concept Map:** Snapshot of the chapter in the form of a graphic organizer for quick recapitulation
- **Keywords:** Definitions of important terms

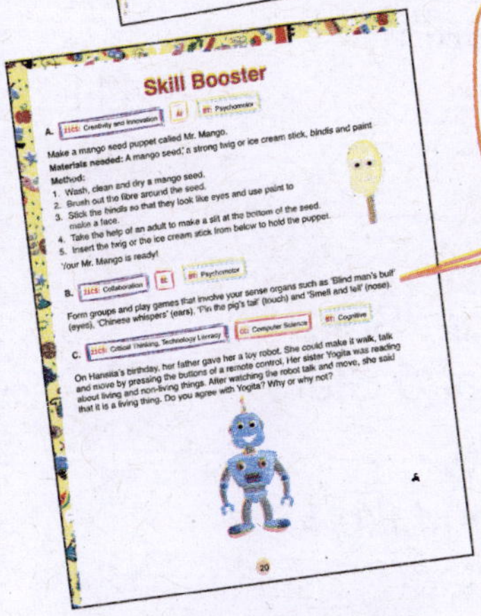

Skill Booster: Section aimed at imparting 21st Century Skills alongwith a focus on Cross-curricular Links, India Focus, Art Integration, Experiential Learning and Bloom's Taxonomy

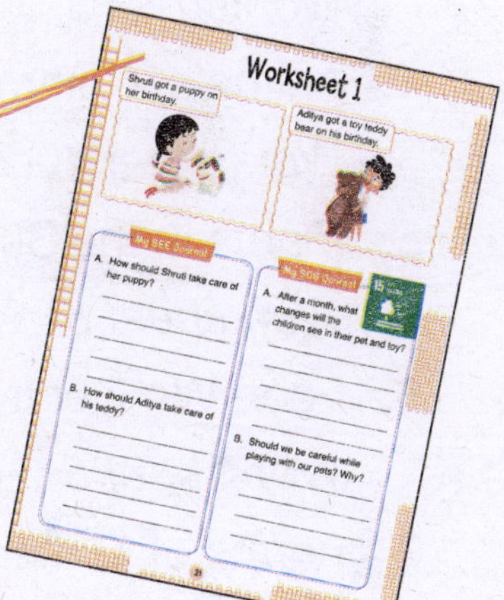

Worksheet: Interesting questions imparting skills catering to social, emotional and ethical (SEE) needs and United Nations' sustainable development goals (SDGs)

My Environment, My Responsibility! (Classes 1 and 2): Special pages to spread awareness and a sense of responsibility towards the environment

Happy Accidents (Classes 3 to 8): Interesting snippets on discoveries and inventions by chance/accidents that led to beneficial ways

STEAM Worksheets (Physics 6 to 8): Interesting project ideas integrating Science, Technology, Engineering, Arts and Mathematics to solve real-world problems

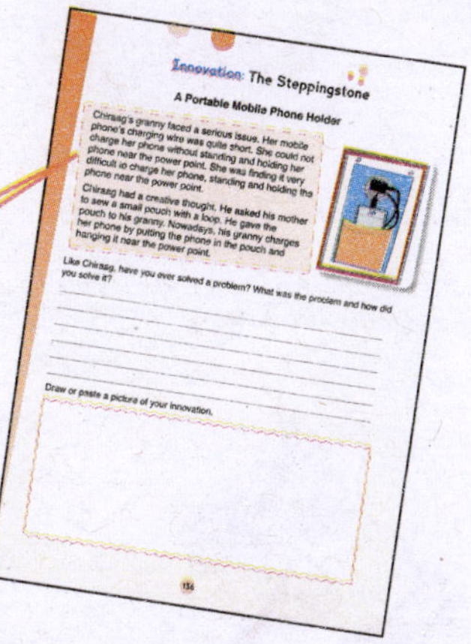

My Eco Craft (Classes 1 and 2): Hands-on activities to enhance learning beyond the classroom

Innovation: The Steppingstone (Classes 3 to 5): Ideas to guide students to solve real-life problems in innovative ways

Role of Science in Benefitting the Society (Classes 6 to 8): Snippets on the contributions made by various scientists for the development of the society

Find Out: Research-oriented questions requiring learners to look beyond the classroom

What do we call the person who treats our pet dog when it falls sick?

FIND OUT

Contents

Be A Scientist! (Classification Activities)

LET'S GET STARTED

We live in a world where amazing things happen around us all the time. Why they happen and how they happen are questions that we often ask.

Let us do an activity to find out what happens when we mix the following ingredients in water.

You will need salt, sugar, coffee powder, rice, dal and five glasses of water.

Predict (guess) what will happen when you put each of these five food items in a glass of water and stir.

Step 1: Add each of the above-mentioned items one by one to a glass of water and stir. Observe what happens. Note your observations. Do they match with what you had guessed?

No.	Food item	Prediction (can see/cannot see the food item)	Observation (can see/cannot see the food item)
1.			
2.			
3.			
4.			
5.			

Step 2: Write in the table below the things that mixed completely in water and the things that did not mix completely in water.

Mixed completely	Did not mix completely

The activity we just did is an example of a simple experiment. Scientists conduct such experiments to find out how things happen.

DO YOU KNOW?

A scientist who studies plants is called a **botanist**.

A scientist who studies animals is called a **zoologist**.

WHO IS A SCIENTIST?

A **scientist** is a person who tries to find out how and why something happens.

You are a scientist if you can:

As a scientist, you can even classify things.

What is the name of the room where scientists carry out their experiments?

FIND OUT

WHAT IS CLASSIFICATION?

Classification means putting things into groups according to their **characteristics**. Scientists classify or sort things based on how things are similar or different.

While classifying or sorting things, we may look at their size, shape, colour, taste, smell, behaviour and habit.

WORD TO KNOW
characteristic: quality of a particular thing

DO IT YOURSELF

A. Classify the given plant parts according to the headings given in the table below.

Broccoli

Beetroot

Tea leaves

Carrots

Cauliflower

Spinach

Mango

Fruit	Flower	Root	Leaf

B. Classify the following animals based on where they live.

crocodile, frog, horse, dolphin, elephant, camel, turtle, fish, whale

Land	Water	Both land and water

C. Classify the following games based on the object required to play them.

chess, badminton, cricket, ludo, tennis, baseball

Board	Bat	Racquet

FAMOUS SCIENTISTS

Acharya Jagadish Chandra Bose was the first person to say that plants too are living things like animals.

Dr A.P.J. Abdul Kalam is known as the 'Missile Man of India'. He also served as the 12th President of India.

Dr C.V. Raman was the first Indian scientist to receive the Nobel Prize in Science.

Homi J. Bhabha is known as the 'Father of the Indian Nuclear Programme'.

TALK TIME

Science makes our lives comfortable. Can you think of three things you use daily that make your life easy?

FIND OUT

What would happen if you get only five minutes to pick up a particular thing from a supermarket where things are kept randomly?

CONCEPT MAP

To Become a Scientist → Predict → Observe → Check and note → Conclude → Report the results

KEYWORDS

Scientist: a person who observes, predicts, experiments, notes and concludes

Classification: grouping or sorting things based on similarities or differences

1 Living and Non-living Things

Prior Knowledge

- Plants and animals around us
- Needs of living things—food, water, air, clothing and shelter

Learning Objectives

- Difference between living and non-living things
- Difference between plants and animals

LET'S GET STARTED

Tick (✔) the living things.

1

Hen

( )

2

Pencil

( )

3

Bird

( )

4

Tree

( )

We see many things around us. Some of them are living, while others are non-living. People, animals and plants are examples of living things. Stones, rocks, mountains and soil are examples of non-living things.

DIFFERENCES BETWEEN LIVING AND NON-LIVING THINGS

Let us see what makes living things different from non-living things.

Living Things Grow

Look at the pictures given below. What do you notice?

A baby grows into an adult.

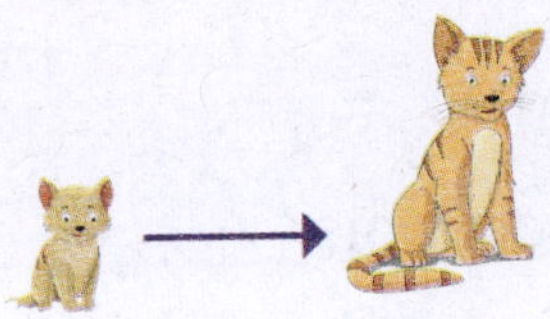

A kitten grows into a cat.

A seedling grows into a plant.

We see that a baby grows into an adult, a kitten into a cat and a sapling (seedling) into a big plant.

Living things **grow** and change their size and shape.

But, do non-living things such as a table or a mobile phone grow? Do they change shape or size?

Non-living things such as cars, tables, chairs and telephones cannot grow or change their size and shape on their own.

Table

Mobile phone

We breathe through our nose.

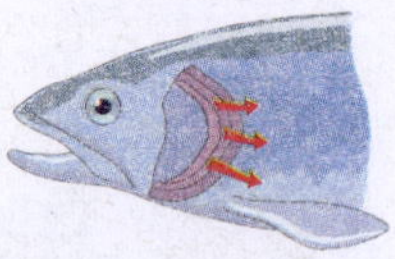

Fish breathe through gills.

Living Things Breathe

Put your hand near your nose. Do you feel the air you are breathing out? (Yes/No)

Now, put your hand close to a doll's nose. Do you feel any air coming out? (Yes/No)

All living things need air to breathe.

- Human beings breathe through their **nose**. Most animals that live on land such as dogs, cows and cats also breathe through their nose.
- Fish breathe through their **gills**.

- Insects breathe through tiny holes on their bodies called **air holes**.
- Some animals such as earthworms breathe through their **skin**.

Insects breathe through air holes.

Earthworms breathe through moist skin.

How Do Plants Breathe?

Plants breathe through tiny pores called **stomata** (singular: stoma) present on the underside of their leaves. Like all living things, plants take in oxygen from the air and give out carbon dioxide while breathing.

Non-living things cannot breathe.

Stoma

DO IT YOURSELF

1. Take two potted plants.
2. Cover one plant with a plastic sheet.
3. Keep both the plants aside for a few days.

You will find that the covered plant dies soon as it does not get air to breathe.

GREENATHON

Grow a plant in a pot on your windowsill or balcony. Remember to water and look after it.

Living Things Move

Living things can move on their own from one place to another.

Plants cannot move from place to place like animals, but they can move some of their parts. A bud blooms to be a flower and the stem of a plant moves towards sunlight.

A boy running

A bird flying

Non-living things cannot move on their own. They need to be lifted or pushed from one place to another.

Cars and buses move only when we drive them.

Living Things Need Food

Living things need food to grow and live. Human beings and animals get their food from plants and other animals.

A bird feeding on an insect

A sheep eating grass

Plants make their food with the help of air, water and sunlight.

Do we ever need to feed our music system or telephone? (Yes/No)

Non-living things do not need food.

> When the leaves of *Mimosa* plants are touched, they curl and close. Find the common name of the plant.
>
> 
>
> **FIND OUT**

Living Things Feel and Respond

All living things can feel and respond to changes around them.

A scared boy running

An injured boy crying

DO YOU KNOW?

A snake feels through its skin!

Animals and human beings feel through their five sense organs—eyes, nose, ears, skin and tongue.

Insects have antennae to sense things around them.

Insects sense things using antennae.

Plants do not have sense organs but can feel and respond to changes around them. Put a potted plant on your windowsill. What do you notice? You would see that the plant bends towards sunlight.

Knock a table with a hammer. Does it feel any pain? (Yes/No)

Non-living things cannot feel.

Plant bends towards sunlight.

QUICK REVISION

Fill in the blanks.

1. Fish have __________ (gills/lungs) to breathe.
2. Living things need __________ (fuel/food) to grow and live.
3. Plants make their food with the help of air, __________ (water/clouds) and sunlight.
4. All living things can __________ (feel/touch) the changes around them.

Living Things Reproduce

Living things produce more living things of their kind. This is called **reproduction**.

Plants produce seeds that grow into new plants. Human beings, dogs, cows, elephants and other animals give birth to young ones that grow into adults.

Seed of a plant produces another plant.

A cow with its calf

A mother with her baby

Birds lay eggs that hatch into baby birds.

Do tables, chairs and pencils have babies? (Yes/No)

Non-living things cannot reproduce.

Hen with its chick

Living Things Have a Lifespan

All living things grow up, grow old and finally die. The time from birth till death is called **lifespan**.

Some living things have a very short lifespan such as a few hours, while others may have a very long lifespan such as 80–90 years.

For how many years does a tortoise live?

FIND OUT

DIFFERENCES BETWEEN ANIMALS AND PLANTS

Both plants and animals are living things, but they are different from each other in some ways.

Animals	Plants
• Animals move from one place to another in search of food and shelter.	• Plants stay in one place and make their food.
• Animals breathe through the nose, gills, air holes or skin.	• Plants breathe through tiny holes called stomata in their leaves.
• Animals have sense organs.	• Plants do not have sense organs.
• Animals reproduce by giving birth to young ones or by laying eggs.	• Plants reproduce through seeds, stems, roots and leaves.

Animals and plants depend on each other. Plants provide food and shelter to animals, while animals help spread the seeds of plants far and wide.

Both work together in harmony to make sure that life on the Earth continues.

DO YOU KNOW?

Non-living things can be natural, such as mountains, rivers, stars and rocks, or artificial, such as cars, toys and pencils.

Clouds move and seem to grow bigger. Yet, they are non-living things. Why?

Fire grows bigger and seems to consume everything as it burns. Then, why is it a non-living thing?

FIND OUT

CONCEPT MAP

Things Around Us

- **Living things**
  - Eat, grow, breathe, move, feel and reproduce
    - Examples: plants and animals
- **Non-living things**
  - Cannot eat, grow, breathe, move, feel and reproduce
    - Examples: tables, books and pencils

KEYWORDS

Living things: things that grow, breathe, move, need food, feel and reproduce

Non-living things: things that cannot grow, breathe, move, eat, feel and reproduce

Stomata: tiny holes on the underside of leaves, which help the plants to breathe

Reproduce: to produce young ones of one's own kind

Sense organs: parts of the body that help us feel changes around us

Exercise

Objective Type Questions

A. Choose the correct answer.

1. Fish breathe through which of the following organs?
   a. Breathing hole b. Gills c. Stomata d. Antennae
2. How many sense organs do we have?
   a. Four b. Six c. Five d. Three
3. Which of the following cannot reproduce?
   a. Whale b. Penguin c. Clock d. Cockroach
4. A cat cannot ______________.
   a. feel b. jump c. make food d. move
5. Plants do not have ______________.
   a. sense organs b. roots c. stems d. leaves

B. Fill in the blanks.

1. A dog breathes through its ______________ (gills/nose).
2. Plants breathe through tiny pores called ______________ (stomata/roots).
3. Insects have ______________ (wings/antennae) to sense things around them.
4. Birds lay ______________ (young ones/eggs) to reproduce.
5. ______________ (Living/Non-living) things can move on their own.

C. Match the following.

1. Cow	a. Gills
2. Cockroach	b. Skin
3. Earthworm	c. Nose
4. Fish	d. Air holes
5. Plant	e. Stomata

D. Write T for True and F for False.

1. We see only living things around us.
2. Soil is a non-living thing.
3. An earthworm breathes through air holes present on its body.
4. Animals make their own food.
5. A hen lays eggs.

Subjective Type Questions

A. Define the following.

1. Stomata
2. Reproduction
3. Lifespan
4. Sense organs
5. Non-living things

B. Answer the following questions in brief.

1. Name the organ human beings use to breathe.
2. Why do living things need food?
3. Name the five sense organs.
4. How does an earthworm breathe?
5. How do plants reproduce?

C. Answer the following questions in detail.

1. Write five differences between living and non-living things.
2. All living things can feel changes around them. Explain how.
3. Write four differences between a dog and a tree.
4. Different living beings breathe through different organs. Explain.
5. How do plants and animals help each other?

Application-based Question

What can a mango tree do that a book cannot do?

Picture-based Questions

Observe the given pictures and answer the questions that follow.

1. Identify the living things that breathe through their nose and colour them in blue.
2. Identify the living things that breathe through stomata and colour them in green.
3. Identify the non-living things and colour them in red.

Skill Booster

A. 21CS: Creativity and Innovation | AI | BT: Psychomotor

Make a mango seed puppet called Mr. Mango.

Materials needed: A mango seed, a strong twig or ice cream stick, *bindis* and paint

Method:

1. Wash, clean and dry a mango seed.
2. Brush out the fibre around the seed.
3. Stick the *bindis* so that they look like eyes and use paint to make a face.
4. Take the help of an adult to make a slit at the bottom of the seed.
5. Insert the twig or the ice cream stick from below to hold the puppet.

Your Mr. Mango is ready!

B. 21CS: Collaboration | EL | BT: Psychomotor

Form groups and play games that involve your sense organs such as 'Blind man's buff' (eyes), 'Chinese whispers' (ears), 'Pin the pig's tail' (touch) and 'Smell and tell' (nose).

C. 21CS: Critical Thinking, Technology Literacy | CC: Computer Science | BT: Cognitive

On Hansita's birthday, her father gave her a toy robot. She could make it walk, talk and move by pressing the buttons of a remote control. Her sister Yogita was reading about living and non-living things. After watching the robot talk and move, she said that it is a living thing. Do you agree with Yogita? Why or why not?

Worksheet 1

Shruti got a puppy on her birthday.

Aditya got a toy teddy bear on his birthday.

My SEE Journal

A. How should Shruti take care of her puppy?

____

____

____

____

____

B. How should Aditya take care of his teddy?

____

____

____

____

____

My SDG Journal

15 LIFE ON LAND

A. After a month, what changes will the children see in their pet and toy?

____

____

____

____

____

B. Should we be careful while playing with our pets? Why?

____

____

____

____

2 Human Body

Prior Knowledge

- Names and functions of different parts of our body
- Our sense organs and their functions
- Keeping body clean and healthy

Learning Objectives

- Internal organs and organ systems
- Functions of different organ systems
- Respiratory system
- Air pollution

LET'S GET STARTED

In Class 2, we have learned that our body is made up of many organs. Write the names of the organs that are shown below using the words given in the box.

stomach   brain   tongue   heart

1. 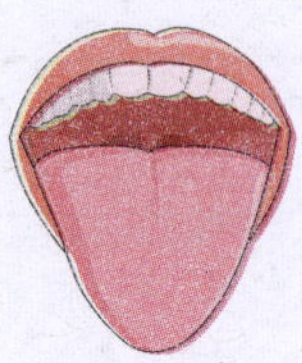 ____________
2. 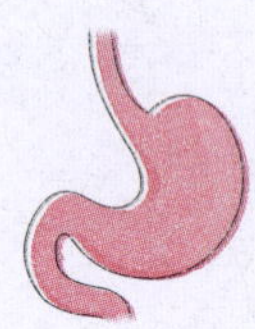 ____________
3. 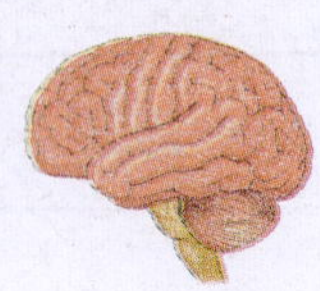 ____________
4. 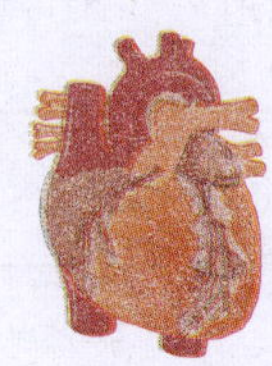 ____________

Our body is made up of tiny units called **cells**. Similar cells together form **tissues**. Different tissues together form an **organ**. Organs that work together to perform a common function form an **organ system**. Many organ systems together form an **organism**.

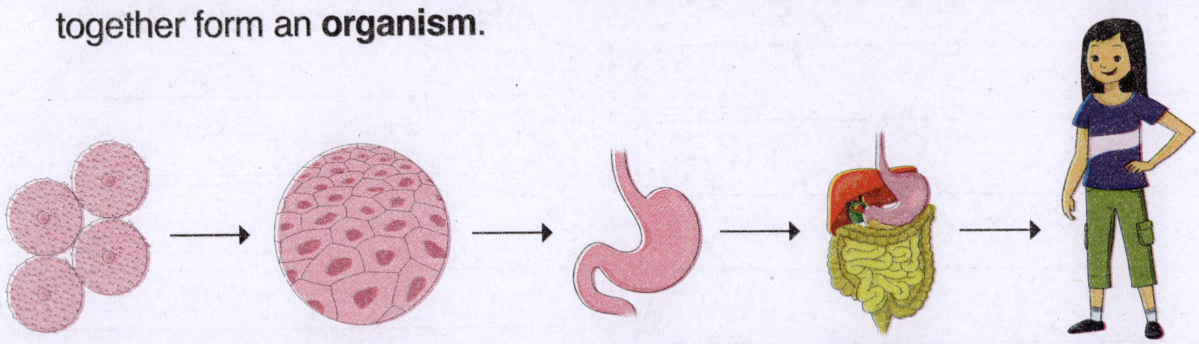

All organ systems work together to keep the body working. Let us learn about some important internal organs and organ systems of our body.

SKELETAL SYSTEM

With your right hand, press your left arm. Do you feel something hard? The hard parts that you feel are our **bones**. There are 206 bones in an adult's body. All the bones in our body together form the **skeletal system**.

The skeletal system gives shape and support to our body and protects the organs inside our body.

The place where two bones meet is called a **joint**. Without the joints, we would not be able to move our body parts in different directions.

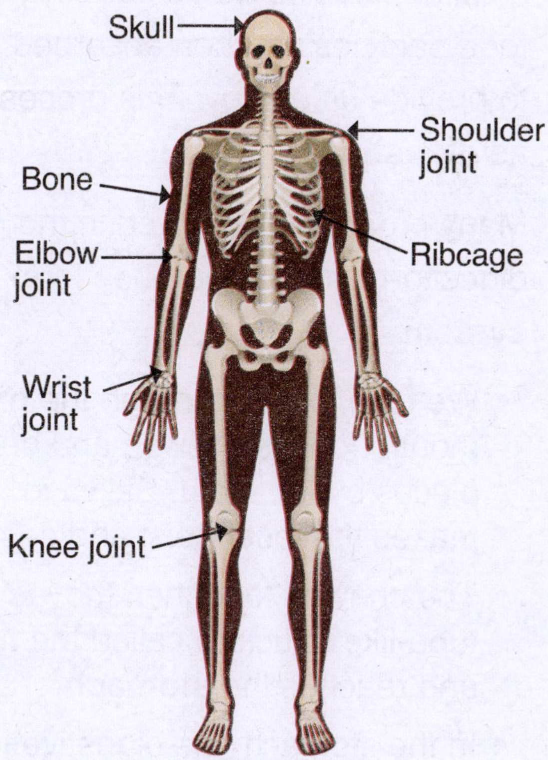

Skeletal system

MUSCULAR SYSTEM

Muscles in our body form the **muscular system**. **Muscles** are attached to bones and together they help us to move. There are about 640 muscles in our body.

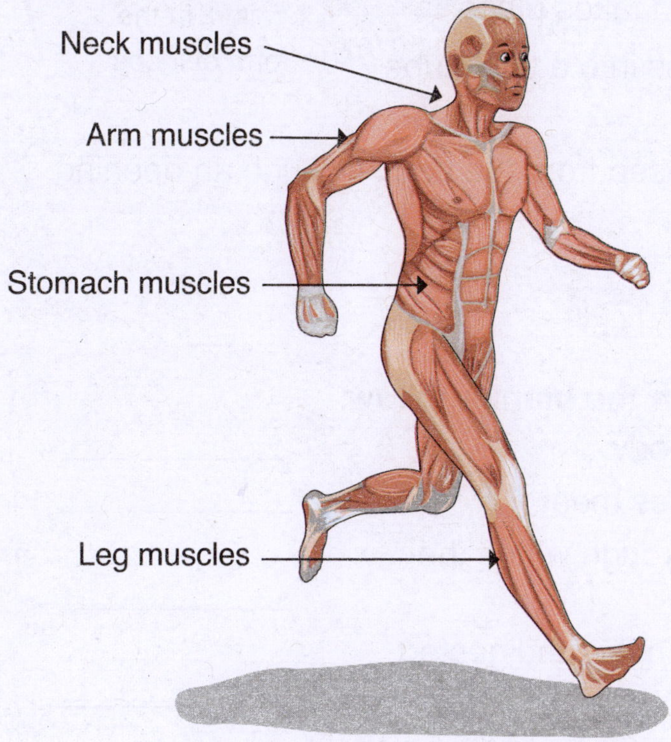

Muscular system

FIND OUT

Find the names of the shortest and the longest bones in our body and the parts in which they are found.

DO YOU KNOW?

The muscles of our heart are the hardest working muscles in our body. They work 24 hours a day.

DIGESTIVE SYSTEM

The food that we eat gets broken down into smaller particles inside our body. The smaller food particles are then absorbed by the body to provide us energy. This process is known as **digestion**.

Many organs are involved in the process of digestion and together they form the **digestive system**.

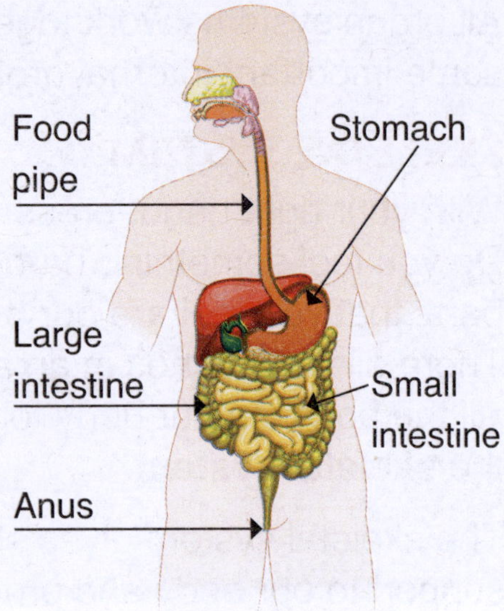

Digestive system

- We take in food through the **mouth**. In the mouth, food is chewed and broken into smaller pieces by the teeth. Saliva in the mouth makes the food moist and easy to swallow.
- The chewed food then moves down a tube-like structure called the **food pipe** and reaches the **stomach**.
- In the stomach, the digestive juices help digest the food.
- From the stomach, the partially digested food reaches a coiled tube-like organ called the **small intestine**. Here, the complete digestion of food takes place.
- The food left undigested then moves into a thick tube called the **large intestine**.
- Finally, the undigested food is released from the body through an opening called the **anus**.

DO YOU KNOW?

The small intestine is 6 m long, while the large intestine is only 1 m long. The large intestine is called so because it is wider than the small intestine.

WORD TO KNOW

coiled: in the form of loops

QUICK REVISION

Who am I? Write the answers in the blanks below.

1. I am the smallest unit of the body. ____________
2. I am the place where two bones meet. ____________
3. I am the tube-like structure through which the food reaches the stomach. ____________
4. I am an opening through which the undigested food is released from the body. ____________

EXCRETORY SYSTEM

The excretory system of our body helps remove waste materials from our body. It consists of the **urinary system**, **lungs** and **skin**.

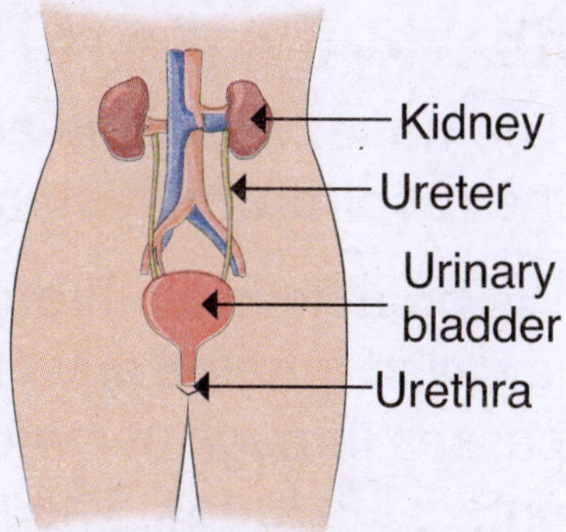

Urinary system

The kidneys, ureters, urinary bladder and urethra form the urinary system. They remove waste in the form of urine from the body.

The lungs help to remove carbon dioxide from the body.

The skin gets rid of excess salt and water from the body through pores in the form of sweat.

NERVOUS SYSTEM

The **brain**, **spinal cord** and **nerves** together form the **nervous system**.

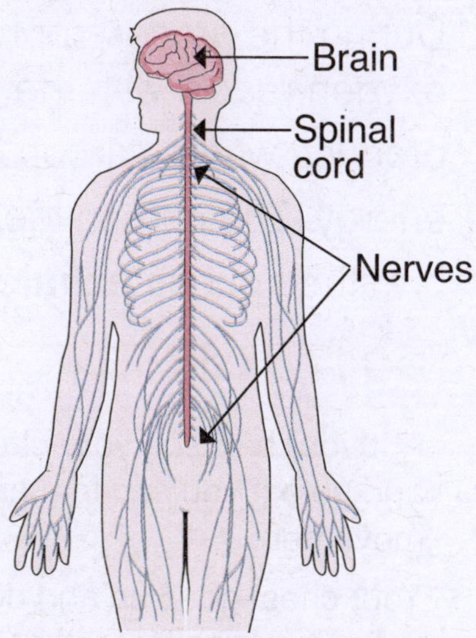

Nervous system

The brain is present inside the head. It controls all our organ systems. Nerves carry messages from the brain to all parts of the body. They also carry messages to the brain. The spinal cord connects the nerves to the brain.

DO YOU KNOW?

When a message reaches the brain from any part of the body, the brain tells the body how to react.

For example, if you touch a hot pan, the nerves in your skin send a message to your brain. The brain then sends a message back, telling the muscles in your hand to pull away. This whole process is done even before you can count to two!

Why is *rajma* called kidney beans?

FIND OUT

CIRCULATORY SYSTEM

The **circulatory system** consists of the **heart**, **blood** and the **blood vessels**.

The heart pumps blood to every part of the body through a network of blood vessels.

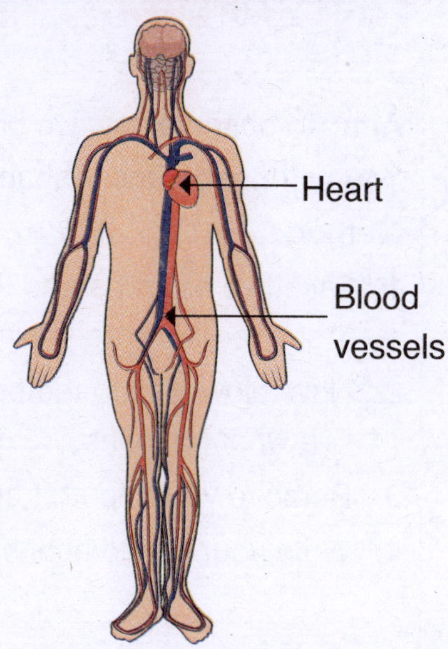

Circulatory system

RESPIRATORY SYSTEM

The **nose**, **windpipe** and **lungs** together form the **respiratory system**.

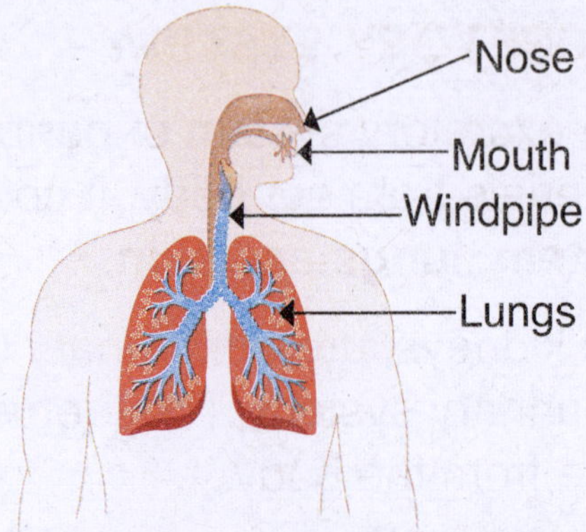

Respiratory system

We breathe in air through our **nose**. This air is called **inhaled air**. The inhaled air then passes through our **windpipe** and finally enters the **lungs**. The lungs take in oxygen from the air.

During the process of respiration, the oxygen reacts with the digested food to produce water, carbon dioxide and energy. The carbon dioxide is then breathed out as **exhaled air**.

FIND OUT

Why do we breathe so heavily after running for sometime?

DO IT YOURSELF

Put your hand on your chest and note if you can feel any movement.

Your chest goes up and down. When we breathe in, the lungs fill up with air and get inflated like a balloon. When we breathe out, the air leaves the lungs and they get deflated, just like a balloon does when air is released from it.

DO YOU KNOW?

- Our lungs are protected by a bony structure called **ribcage**.
- When we inhale, the oxygen from the air is taken in by our lungs. The blood vessels in the lung then carry it to all the parts of our body.
- Our body parts use oxygen to perform their actions. In doing so, they produce carbon dioxide as a waste. The blood vessels carry the carbon dioxide back to the lungs, from where it is exhaled.

ACTIVITY 1

Aim: To observe how we breathe

You will need: One Y-shaped tube, two big balloons and a sellotape

Method:

1. Take two balloons and tie them firmly at the two ends of the Y-shaped tube, as shown in the picture.
2. Now, blow air into the open end of the tube with your mouth and see what happens.
3. Remove your mouth from the tube and see what happens.
4. Write your observations here.

____

____

AIR POLLUTION

The addition of harmful substances to the environment reduces the quality of the air around us. This is called **air pollution**.

Causes of Air Pollution

Some causes of air pollution are given below:

Smoke from vehicles and factories

- The smoke from vehicles, factories and industries pollutes the air.
- Use of coal, wood and kerosene as fuel also causes air pollution.
- Burning of crackers, rubber tyres and other waste materials also adds to the pollution.
- Air pollution is also caused by dust storms and strong winds.

Effects of Air Pollution

The main effects of air pollution are given below:

- Breathing polluted air may cause respiratory diseases and breathing problems such as asthma.
- Dusty air could be a carrier of germs and can cause severe eye infections.
- Dust particles could also enter our nose causing irritation.

Ways to Reduce Air Pollution

Some steps that can be taken to reduce air pollution are given below:

- We should walk or cycle short distances instead of using a vehicle.
- The gases and smoke from factories should be filtered before releasing them from chimneys.
- Factories should be constructed far away from areas where people live.
- We should plant more trees and stop cutting down trees.

CONCEPT MAP

Organ Systems

Skeletal system	Muscular system	Digestive system	Respiratory system	Excretory system	Nervous system	Circulatory system
Bones	Muscles	Mouth Food pipe Stomach Small intestine Large intestine Anus	Nose Windpipe Lungs	Kidneys Ureters Urinary bladder Urethra Skin Lungs	Brain Nerves Spinal cord	Heart Blood Blood vessels

KEYWORDS

Cells: tiny units that are the building blocks of our body

Tissue: a group of similar cells

Organ: a group of tissues working together

Organ system: a group of organs performing one function together

Bones: the hard parts of our body

Joint: the place where two bones meet

Nerves: the structures that carry messages between the brain and all other parts of the body

Spinal cord: the organ that connects the nerves to the brain

Blood vessels: thin tubes through which blood flows between different parts of the body

Inhaled air: the air we breathe in

Exhaled air: the air we breathe out

Air pollution: the decrease in the quality of the air around us due to the addition of harmful substances to the environment

Exercise

Objective Type Questions

A. Choose the correct answer.

1. ______________ system is not a human body system.
   a. Respiratory b. Thinking c. Digestive d. Circulatory
2. Without the ______________ system, we would be shapeless.
   a. excretory b. skeletal c. circulatory d. respiratory
3. The ______________ is not a part of the digestive system.
   a. windpipe b. mouth c. anus d. stomach
4. The ______________ pumps blood to every part of the body.
   a. lungs b. heart c. brain d. stomach
5. Nerves are a part of the ______________ system.
   a. circulatory b. excretory c. nervous d. digestive

B. Write T for True and F for False.

1. We have 206 muscles.
2. The small intestine is longer than the large intestine.
3. We breathe in air through our ears.
4. Kidneys help us to get rid of sweat.
5. Blood is pumped to every part of our body through nerves.

C. Match the following.

1. Brain	a. Respiratory system
2. Kidney	b. Muscular system
3. Windpipe	c. Skeletal system
4. Muscles	d. Nervous system
5. Skull	e. Digestive system
6. Small intestine	f. Excretory system

D. Give two examples for each of the following.

1. Organs of the digestive system ______________ ______________
2. Organs of the respiratory system ______________ ______________
3. Organs of the nervous system ______________ ______________
4. Organs of the circulatory system ______________ ______________
5. Organs of the excretory system ______________ ______________

Subjective Type Questions

A. Define the following.

1. Organ systems 2. Joint 3. Small intestine
4. Nerves 5. Air pollution

B. Answer the following questions in brief.

1. What are cells?
2. What is the role of muscles in our body?
3. What is digestion?
4. Name the main organs of the circulatory system.
5. List the main organs of the excretory system.

C. Answer the following questions in detail.

1. How does the skeletal system help us?
2. Name and draw the organs of the digestive system.
3. How does the body get rid of waste materials?
4. Name the organs of the nervous system and explain how they work together.
5. List two steps we can take to reduce air pollution.

Application-based Questions

A. Which is the most important organ in our body and why?

B. Which body systems are involved when we eat?

Picture-based Question

Name the organ systems that help you to do the following things.

Skill Booster

A. **21CS:** Information Literacy | **CC:** General Knowledge | **BT:** Cognitive

We must keep our body protected from germs and diseases. Which of the following will keep you healthy? Tick (✔) the correct statements.

- Running and playing
- Eating only chips and burgers
- Not opening the windows of your room
- Drinking plenty of water
- Doing yoga

B. **21CS:** Flexibility and Adaptability | **CC:** General Knowledge | **BT:** Cognitive, Affective

Some people are different—they may not have all the body systems functioning properly. But that does not stop them from being successful. Examples of some such famous people are Helen Keller, Sudha Chandran and Beethoven. Find out why they are famous.

Worksheet 2

My SEE Journal

A. How can Pooja take care of her teeth?

____

____

____

____

____

B. What should Pooja do to stay healthy?

____

____

____

____

____

My SDG Journal

3 GOOD HEALTH AND WELL-BEING

A. Why should Pooja start taking care of her health from a young age?

____

____

____

____

____

B. What should you do everyday to keep your body healthy and fit?

____

____

____

____

3 Animals: Birds

Prior Knowledge

- Names of birds around us
- Characteristics of birds

Learning Objectives

- How does a bird fly?
- Feathers and beaks
- Feet and claws
- Nests

LET'S GET STARTED

We see many types of birds around us. Given below are some questions about birds. Tick the correct option. Look at the pictures given below as hint.

1. Which is the largest bird in the world?

   a. Emu ◯ b. Penguin ◯ c. Ostrich ◯

2. Which of these birds has a huge beak to drink water?

   a. Pelican ◯ b. Stork ◯ c. Emu ◯

3. Which of these is a night bird?

   a. Bat ◯ b. Owl ◯ c. Peacock ◯

4. Which of these is a large bird with a hooked beak and sharp claws?

   a. Parrot ◯ b. Hen ◯ c. Vulture ◯

Owl

Vulture

Pelican

Ostrich

Birds are of various shapes and colours. We see them flying in the sky, **perching** on trees and sometimes swimming in water.

WORD TO KNOW
perch: to sit, rest or balance

WHAT HELPS A BIRD TO FLY?

Birds can fly with the help of their wings. They have:

- strong muscles to move their wings
- light feathers
- light, hollow bones
- streamlined or boat-shaped body
- a tail that helps them to change directions

Upstroke

Downstroke

HOW DOES A BIRD FLY?

A bird moves its wings to fly and lift itself up in the air. It flaps its wings upwards and downwards. The upward and backward movement is called **upstroke**. The downward flapping of wings is called **downstroke**. When the bird has to land, it spreads its wings and glides down without flapping its wings too much.

DO YOU KNOW?

Many birds fly thousands of kilometres every year in search of food and better climate or to lay eggs. This is called **migration**. The Arctic Tern travels from the Arctic region to Antarctica every year and then goes back.

Flightless Birds

Most birds can fly. But there are some birds such as ostrich, kiwi, emu and penguin that cannot fly.

Emu

Ostrich

Penguin

TALK TIME

Why do you think ostrich and emu cannot fly?

FEATHERS

Feathers cover the body of birds. They make the birds different from all other living things. Feathers help birds fly, keep their body warm and give them shape.

DO YOU KNOW?

The scientific study of birds is called **ornithology**.

Birds have three kinds of feathers:

- **Flight feathers**: These are strong feathers on the wings and the tail.
- **Down feathers**: These are soft feathers that keep the birds' body warm.
- **Body feathers**: These feathers cover the body of birds and give them shape.

Flight feather

Down feather

Body feather

BEAKS

Birds do not have teeth. They eat with the help of their beaks. Depending upon the food they eat, birds have different kinds of beaks.

Parrot

Hoopoe

Parrots have a **short, curved** beak to crack nuts and seeds.

Hoopoes have a **long, slender** beak to pick up insects from holes in the ground.

Hummingbird

Sunbird

Hummingbirds and sunbirds have **long, pointed** and **straw-like** beaks to suck nectar from flowers.

Ducks and spoonbills have **flat, broad** beaks with holes along the edges. These holes allow water to flow out, leaving behind tiny water creatures and plants in the birds' mouth.

Eagles, owls, hawks and falcons have **sharp, hooked** beaks to tear flesh. Cranes, herons and storks have **long, pointed** beaks to catch fish.

Sparrow and pigeons have **short, hard** and **strong** beaks to help them crush grains and seeds.

Woodpeckers have a **sharp, pointed** beak that helps them to make holes in tree trunks to pull out insects.

Duck

Eagle

Sparrow

Woodpecker

QUICK REVISION

Give one example of a bird that has the following kinds of beaks.

1. Long, slender beak: ____________
2. Flat, broad beak: ____________
3. Sharp, hooked beak: ____________
4. Short, hard and strong beak: ____________
5. Long, pointed and straw-like beak: ____________

FEET AND CLAWS

Birds use their feet and claws to catch food, sit on branches of trees and protect themselves. Most birds have four toes on each foot. At the end of the toe is the claw, which looks like a sharp nail.

Toes of a crow

Perching Birds

Sparrow, crow and myna have slender toes. They have three toes in front and one at the back. They use their toes to grip branches and wires while sitting like we use our fingers and thumbs to grip objects.

Toes of a hen

Scratching Birds

Hens, peacocks and roosters scratch or dig the ground with their toes to find insects and worms to eat.

Toes of a woodpecker

Climbing Birds

Woodpeckers and parrots have two toes in the front and two toes at the back. This helps them to climb and cling to trees.

Swimming Birds

Gooses and ducks have three toes in the front joined with skin in the form of a web. These webbed feet help them swim.

Webbed toes of a duck

Wading Birds

Storks, cranes and herons have long, slender legs with widespread toes to keep their feet from sinking in the soft mud. They walk in shallow water in search of food.

WORD TO KNOW

wade: to walk through water

Long legs of a crane

Flesh-eating or Preying Birds

Hawks, eagles, vultures and falcons have strong, sharp, curved claws called **talons** to catch and hold their prey such as rat, frog and snake.

Claws of a vulture

DO YOU KNOW?

Kingfishers like to eat fish, but some of them eat insects, frogs, worms, spiders and even snakes!

NESTS

Birds build nests to lay eggs and raise their **nestlings**. Once the baby birds are old enough to look after themselves, they leave the nest, never to return.

Mother bird feeding its young ones in their nest.

WORD TO KNOW

nestlings: baby birds

Nests can be small or big. Birds may build their nests on tree tops, on the ground or on the roofs of houses.

Birds build nests with various materials such as twigs, dry leaves, grass, cotton, feathers, straw, wool and even a piece of rag.

Woodpecker making its nest

Weaverbird making its nest

Different Kinds of Nests Built by Birds

A woodpecker makes a hole in the bark of a tree with its beak and uses it as a nest.

The weaverbird uses its beak to weave leaves and twigs to make its nest. Unlike other nests, the weaverbird's nest has an opening from the bottom.

DO YOU KNOW?

Dr Salim Ali, an Indian ornithologist is known as the 'Birdman of India'. He has studied many birds and written many books on them.

The tailorbird uses its beak like a needle and stitches the leaves to make its nest. It uses wool, cotton thread or the thread of a spider's web to stitch its nest.

Eagles normally build their nest high up on cliffs or tall trees to protect their eggs.

Penguins build their nest with stones and pebbles.

Tailorbird making its nest

Eagle's nest

The cuckoo is a lazy bird and does not make its own nest. Instead, it lays its eggs in a crow's nest. As the eggs look similar to a crow's eggs, the crow looks after the cuckoo's eggs as its own.

Penguin's nest

DO IT YOURSELF

Take a big plastic bowl. Fill it with water and keep it in your garden or on the windowsill. Enjoy seeing the birds coming and taking a dip in the bird bath.

CONCEPT MAP

Types of Beaks

- Short, curved → Parrot
- Long, slender → Hoopoe
- Long, pointed, straw-like → Sunbird
- Flat, broad with holes → Duck
- Sharp, hooked → Eagle
- Long, pointed → Crane
- Short, hard, strong → Sparrow
- Sharp, pointed → Woodpecker

Uses of Feet and Claws

- Perching → Crow
- Scratching → Hen
- Climbing → Woodpecker
- Swimming → Goose
- Wading → Stork
- Preying → Vulture

KEYWORDS

Upstroke: the upward flapping of wings

Downstroke: the downward flapping of wings

Talons: sharp, curved claws of flesh-eating birds

Exercise

Objective Type Questions

A. Choose the correct answer.

1. The feathers that help a bird to fly are ______________ feathers.
   a. down   b. body   c. flight   d. tail
2. A woodpecker has a ______________ beak.
   a. pointed   b. short   c. flat   d. curved
3. Most birds have ______________ on each foot.
   a. two toes   b. three toes   c. four toes   d. six toes
4. A sparrow is a ______________ bird.
   a. climbing   b. scratching   c. perching   d. swimming
5. The webbed feet of a ______________ help it to swim.
   a. peacock   b. parrot   c. duck   d. eagle

B. Fill in the blanks.

1. The upward and backward movement of a bird's wing is called ______________ (upstroke/downstroke) and the downward movement is called ______________ (upstroke/downstroke).
2. ______________ (Flight/Down) feathers keep a bird's body warm.
3. Eagles have ______________ (long/sharp) and ______________ (flat/hooked) beaks to tear flesh.
4. ______________ (Penguin/Crane) and ______________ (stork/parrot) are wading birds.
5. Hawks have claws called ______________ (fingers/talons) to catch and hold their prey.

C. Match the following.

Toes

1. 

2. 

3. 

4. 

Birds   a. Duck   b. Crow   c. Hen   d. Woodpecker

D. Write T for True and F for False.

1. When a bird has to land, it closes its wings.
2. A kiwi cannot fly.
3. A parrot has a hooked beak to tear flesh.
4. A woodpecker has two toes in the front and two toes at the back.
5. A cuckoo does not make its own nest.

Subjective Type Questions

A. Differentiate between the following.

1. Upstroke and downstroke
2. Body feathers and down feathers
3. Perching birds and scratching birds
4. Climbing birds and swimming birds
5. Wading birds and preying birds

B. Answer the following questions in brief.

1. What helps a bird fly?
2. What are down feathers?
3. What kind of beak does a woodpecker have?
4. What kind of feet do climbing birds have? Draw the feet of any climbing bird.
5. Why do birds build nests?

C. Answer the following questions in detail.

1. How does a bird fly?
2. Name the three types of feathers and their uses. Draw and label the three types of feathers.
3. How does a duck's beak help it to find its food?
4. What is special about the claws of a hawk?
5. How does a tailorbird make its nest?

Application-based Questions

A. How are the toes of perching birds similar to our fingers and thumb?

B. What makes birds different from other animals?

C. After a heavy storm, you find a baby bird on your balcony. It has hurt its wings and cannot fly. How do you think you can take care of it?
Tick (✔) the correct statements.

1. Put it in a cage.
2. Apply medicine to the hurt area.
3. Call the Animal Society to take it away.

Picture-based Question

Trace the dotted line and colour the bird. Can you identify the bird? Write two features of its beak in the space provided.

This bird is ________________.

It has a ________________ and ________________ beak.

Skill Booster

A. 21CS: Creativity and Innovation | AI | BT: Psychomotor

Use twigs or sticks to make a nest. Line it with soft materials such as dry leaves, grass, wool, feathers and straw. Put some white table tennis balls or chocolate eggs to make it look real!

B. 21CS: Critical Thinking | BT: Cognitive, Affective

Rohit and Rahul are good friends. Rohit wants a bird as a birthday gift from his parents. Rahul says that Rohit should not keep a bird locked up in a cage. Do you think Rahul is right? Why or why not?

C. 21CS: Critical Thinking, Collaboration | BT: Cognitive, Affective

One day, while eating grains, little Chicky ate a pea grain by mistake. It got stuck in his throat and he started to cry. The mother hen tried to get the pea out, but her beak was short and she could not reach inside Chicky's throat.

She decided to take help from the neighbour birds. Who do you think will be able to help Chicky and why?

Parrot

Sunbird

Duck

Eagle

D. 21CS: Communication | CC: English | BT: Cognitive, Psychomotor

Write a story titled 'The Bird That Couldn't Stop Talking'. Find out some words that will help you write the story. Do not forget to draw your bird.

Worksheet 3

Noblemen used falcons to hunt in olden days.

In olden times, pigeons were used to carry messages over long distances.

My SEE Journal

A. Ridhi wanted to keep a parrot as a pet. She asked the owner of the pet store about how she should take care of her pet. What do you think the owner told her to do?

____

____

____

____

____

B. Would you like to keep a bird as a pet? If so, which bird would you like? How would you take care of it?

____

____

____

____

My SDG Journal

15 LIFE ON LAND

A. By observing which animal were humans (or scientists) able to manufacture aircraft?

____

____

____

____

____

B. Which birds help to keep the Earth clean and how?

____

____

____

____

____

4 Animals: Common Insects

Prior Knowledge

- Names of insects around us
- Common features of an insect

Learning Objectives

- Body parts of an insect
- Life cycle of insects
- Useful and harmful insects
- Protection from harmful insects

LET'S GET STARTED

Look at the pictures given below. Have you seen these insects? Where have you seen them? Can you name them?

1

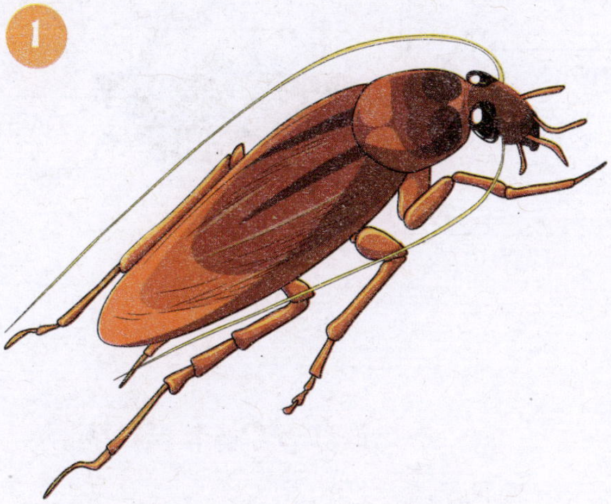

____

2

____

Insects are small creatures that are found everywhere around us. Some of them are useful for us, while some harm us. In this chapter, let us learn about some common insects and their characteristics.

COMMON INSECTS

Some examples of common insects are ladybird, dragonfly, ant, grasshopper and mosquito.

Ladybird

Dragonfly

Ladybirds are small insects and are commonly yellow, orange or **scarlet** with small black spots on their wings. They are commonly found on plants in gardens or fields.

Grasshopper

Dragonflies are flying insects and are usually found around lakes, ponds and wetlands. They have large, transparent wings.

Grasshoppers are medium to large insects. The colour of their body is usually a combination of brown, grey or green, to blend in their environment.

WORD TO KNOW
scarlet: a bright red colour

Body Parts of an Insect

The body of an insect is divided into three main parts: **head**, **thorax** and **abdomen**.

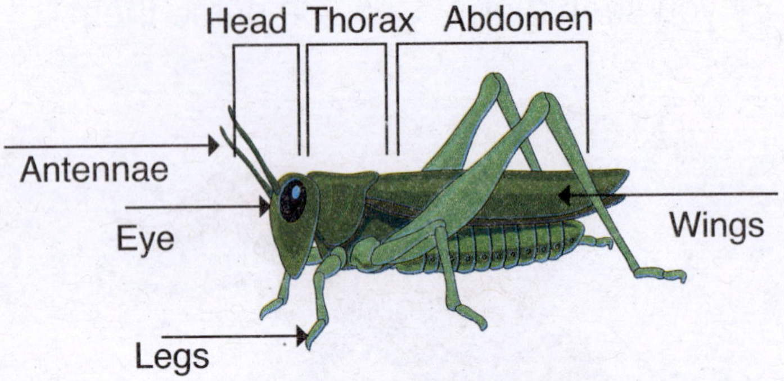

Body parts of an insect

Head: The head of an insect has two eyes, two antennae (singular: antenna) and a mouth. The antennae help the insects to smell, taste and hear. The structure of the mouth varies among different insects depending upon the kind of food they eat.

Thorax: The thorax is the middle part of an insect's body. It is composed of three segments. Each segment has a pair of legs. In insects that fly, the thorax also has wings.

DO YOU KNOW?
Spiders are not insects as they have eight legs. Not all spiders spin a web and wait for their prey to get caught in it. Some of them can catch their prey without the use of web. They are called hunting spiders.

Abdomen: The abdomen is the largest part of an insect's body. It contains the heart and the organs for breathing and digestion.

LIFE CYCLE OF AN INSECT

Insects such as butterflies and houseflies have four stages in their life cycle: egg, larva (plural: larvae) or caterpillar, pupa and adult. However, insects such as grasshoppers and cockroaches have only three stages.

Life Cycle of a Butterfly

Life cycle of a butterfly

A butterfly has four stages in its life cycle. A female butterfly usually lays **eggs** on the underside (bottom side) of a leaf. When an egg hatches, a larva called **caterpillar** comes out. It looks like a worm with many legs. The caterpillar grows in size by eating the leaves of plants. A caterpillar **moults** many times before it changes into a **pupa**. A hard case called a **cocoon** covers the pupa. Inside the cocoon, the body of the pupa changes completely and when the case breaks, a beautiful **adult** butterfly comes out.

> **WORD TO KNOW**
> moult: to shed old skin for new to grow

QUICK REVISION

Who am I?

1. I have six legs. __________
2. I am the largest body part of an insect. __________
3. I am the larva of a butterfly. __________
4. I cover the pupa. __________

USEFUL INSECTS (SOCIAL INSECTS)

Some insects such as bees, ants and butterflies are useful to us. Bees and butterflies fly from flower to flower and help in **pollination**. Ants are **scavengers**.

Ants and bees are social insects, which means they live in large colonies or groups. Ants can be found inside as well as outside our homes.

Bees live in hives that they build in places such as cavities of trees or on rocks. They suck nectar from flowers and therefore help in pollination. They also provide us with honey.

WORDS TO KNOW

pollination: the process that helps plants to produce new seeds

scavengers: animals who feed on dead animals

DO YOU KNOW?

An ant can lift 20 times its own body weight.

Ant feeding on a dead insect

Bees on a honeycomb

HARMFUL INSECTS

Some insects spread disease-causing germs and make us fall sick. Mosquitoes spread diseases such as malaria and dengue. Lice and bedbugs that suck blood make our skin sore and itchy. Cockroaches and houseflies too spread diseases. Termites damage walls, wooden doors, window frames and furniture.

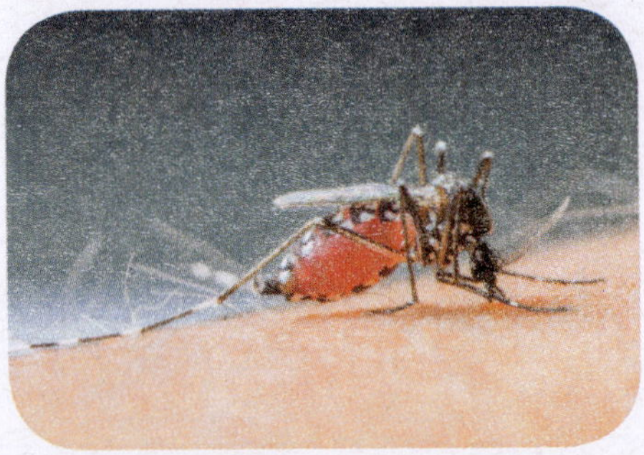

A mosquito sucking blood

A louse

Some insects damage plants and cause harm to animals. Insects such as locusts destroy crops. Fleas and ticks suck blood from the bodies of animals, causing pain and diseases.

1. Who is he?
2. What is he doing and why?

FIND OUT

Protection from Harmful Insects (Remedies)

- We must keep our bodies clean to keep insects away.
- We should use mosquito nets, wire netting on windows and repellents to keep mosquitoes away.
- We can also use insect repellents or mosquito coils to keep insects or mosquitoes away.
- We should not allow water to stagnate, as mosquitoes lay eggs in **stagnant** water.
- We must keep our surroundings clean by throwing the garbage in dustbins.
- We should keep the food covered.
- We must remember to wash and bathe our pet animals to keep them away from ticks and fleas.
- When insects attack trees and plants, we need to use chemicals called **pesticides** to get rid of the pests.

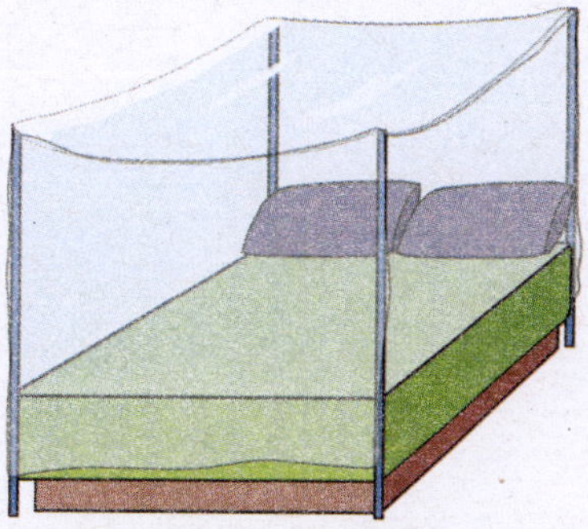

Use mosquito nets

Wire netting on window

Clean surroundings

Cover food and water

WORD TO KNOW

stagnant: a thing standing still or without any flow

CONCEPT MAP

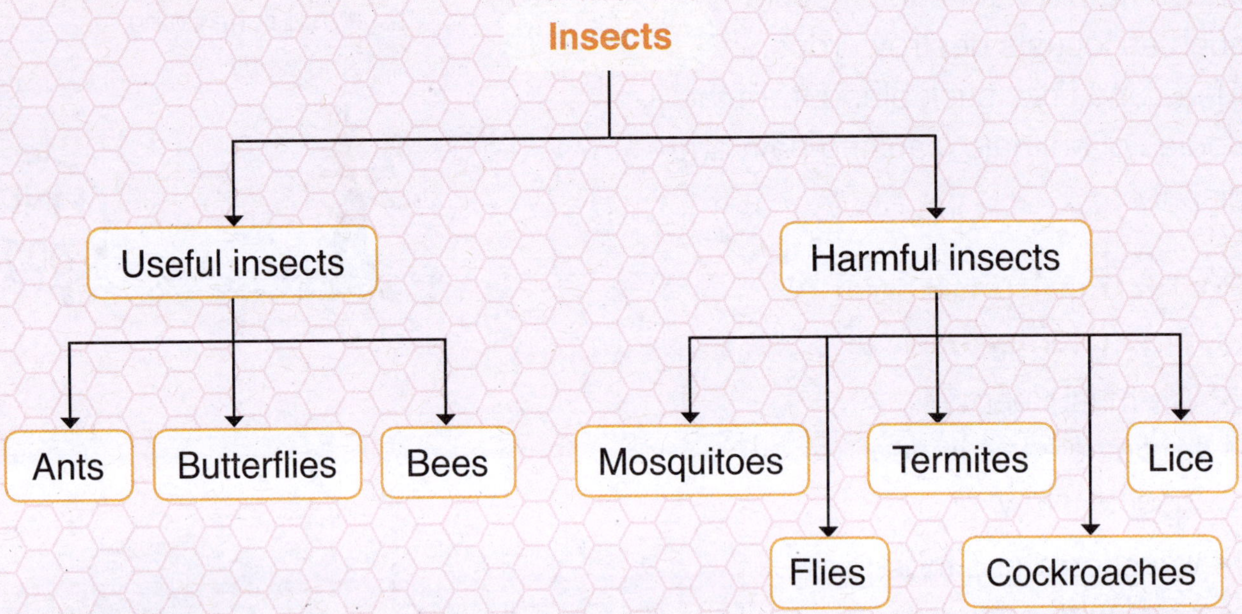

KEYWORDS

Head, thorax and abdomen: the three main body parts of an insect

Social insects: insects that live in groups or colonies

Caterpillar: larva of a butterfly that hatches out of an egg

Pupa: the stage of development between a larva and an adult butterfly

Cocoon: a hard case covering the pupa

Pesticides: the chemicals that keep plants free from harmful insects

Exercise

Objective Type Questions

A. Choose the correct answer.

1. Larva is another name for ______________.
   a. caterpillar b. pupa c. cocoon d. egg
2. A butterfly has ______________ stages in its life cycle.
   a. three b. four c. five d. six
3. Insects have ______________ pairs of legs.
   a. three b. four c. six d. five
4. ______________ is not a main body part of an insect.
   a. Head b. Tail c. Thorax d. Abdomen
5. Which of the following is a social insect?
   a. Mosquito b. Housefly c. Butterfly d. Ant

B. Fill in the blanks.

1. A bedbug is a ______________ (useful/harmful) insect.
2. The wings are attached to the ______________ (head/thorax) of an insect.
3. ______________ (Termites/Bedbugs) suck blood, making our skin sore and itchy.
4. When insects attack trees and plants, we use ______________ (insect repellents/chemical pesticides) to get rid of them.
5. ______________ (Mosquitoes/Butterflies) spread malaria and dengue.

C. Match the following.

1. Bees	a. Destroy crops
2. Butterflies	b. Give us honey
3. Ants	c. Cocoon
4. Locusts	d. Scavengers

D. Write T for True and F for False.

1. Grasshoppers have a body colour to blend in with their environment.
2. Each segment of the thorax has two pairs of legs.
3. The life cycle of a cockroach has three stages.
4. A caterpillar eats the leaves of plants.
5. Butterflies live in large colonies.

Subjective Type Questions

A. Define the following.

1. Thorax
2. Caterpillar
3. Cocoon
4. Moulting

B. Answer the following questions in brief.

1. List the main body parts of an insect.
2. Where do mosquitoes breed?
3. Name any two useful insects.
4. What are social insects? Give two examples.
5. Name one harmful insect for each of the following.

   a. plants b. animals c. humans

C. Answer the following questions in detail.

1. Describe the life cycle of a butterfly with the help of a labelled diagram.
2. How do some insects help us?
3. How are some insects harmful to us?
4. Write four ways in which you can protect yourself from harmful insects.

Application-based Question

Often there are announcements on the radio and TV that we should not allow water to collect in open pots, rubber tubes or any vessel in and around our homes. Why do you think we need to follow this instruction?

Picture-based Question

Label the body parts of an insect in the image given below.

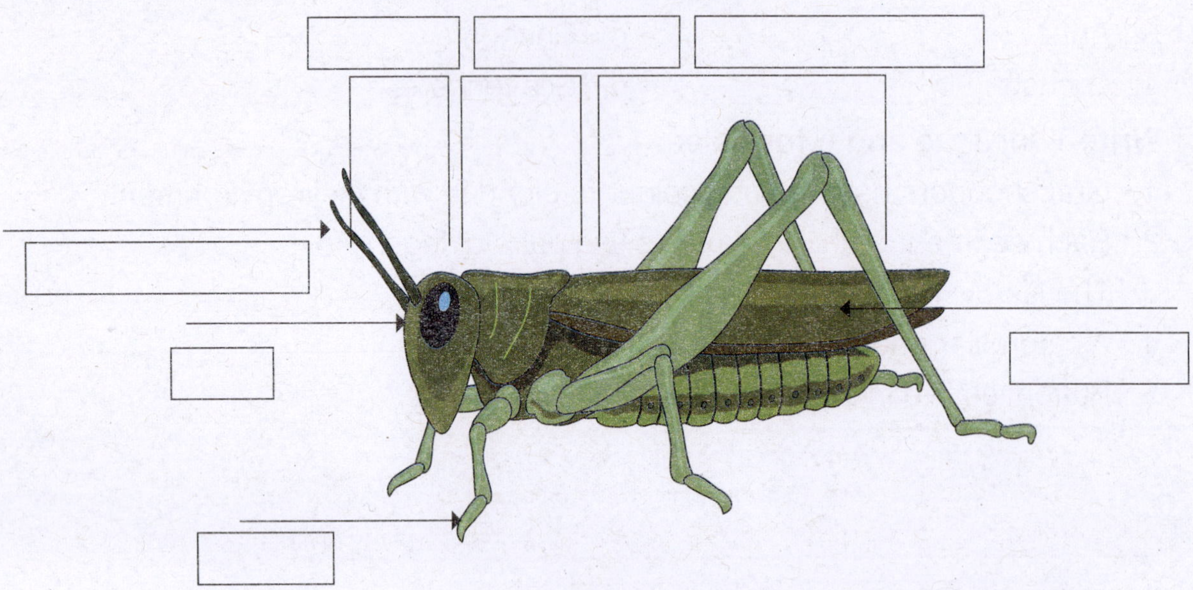

Skill Booster

A. **21CS:** Information Literacy | **CC:** General Knowledge | **BT:** Cognitive, Psychomotor

Find out about two harmful insects and one useful insect that are not mentioned in the chapter. Paste a picture and share the information with your friends.

B. **21CS:** Creativity and Innovation | **AI** | **BT:** Psychomotor

Make an outline of your palms on a sheet of paper of your choice. Paste them as shown in the picture and decorate using ribbons and buttons. Use ribbons or strips of coloured paper to make the feelers and use glue to paste them. Paste colourful buttons of different shapes and sizes to make the body parts of your butterfly.

C. **21CS:** Collaboration, Social and Cross-cultural Interaction | **EL** | **BT:** Affective

Ants are social insects. They live in large colonies or groups. They work together to capture prey. Don't you think we can learn quite a lot from their teamwork behaviour? Discuss this in groups in your class.

Worksheet 4

The ants are having a party with the cookie crumbs Vishal had left while eating.

My SEE Journal

A. What can we learn from the ants?

____

____

____

____

____

____

B. Which qualities of the ants can you include in your life?

____

____

____

____

My SDG Journal

15 LIFE ON LAND

A. Why were there ants near the windowsill?

____

____

____

B. What were the ants doing with the crumbs?

____

____

____

C. Why were the ants carrying away the crumbs instead of eating them there?

____

____

____

5 Plants in the Surroundings

Prior Knowledge

- Different types of plants
- How plants are useful to us

Learning Objectives

- Parts of a plant and their functions
- Structure of a seed
- Germination of seeds

LET'S GET STARTED

In Class 2, we learned about different types of plants—climbers, shrubs, creepers, herbs and trees. Identify the types of plants from the examples given below.

1 

Pumpkin

____

2 

Mango

____

3 

Mint

____

4 

Hibiscus

____

5 

Bitter gourd

____

Our Mother Nature has different types of plants. Plants are found everywhere—on land as well as in water. Different plants have different characteristics. They are useful to us in many ways.

PARTS OF A PLANT

Just as we have different parts in our body, plants also have different parts. Each part has its own function such as making food, absorbing water or helping the plant to grow. Let us learn about the different parts of a plant and their functions.

Every plant has two main parts: the **root system** and the **shoot system**.

DO IT YOURSELF

With the help of an elder, carefully pull out a small plant from the soil, ensuring you do not damage it. Now, observe the different parts of the plant. Remember to plant it back in the soil after observing.

Shoot System:
The part of a plant that grows above the ground is called the shoot system. It consists of a stem, branches, leaves, flowers and fruits.

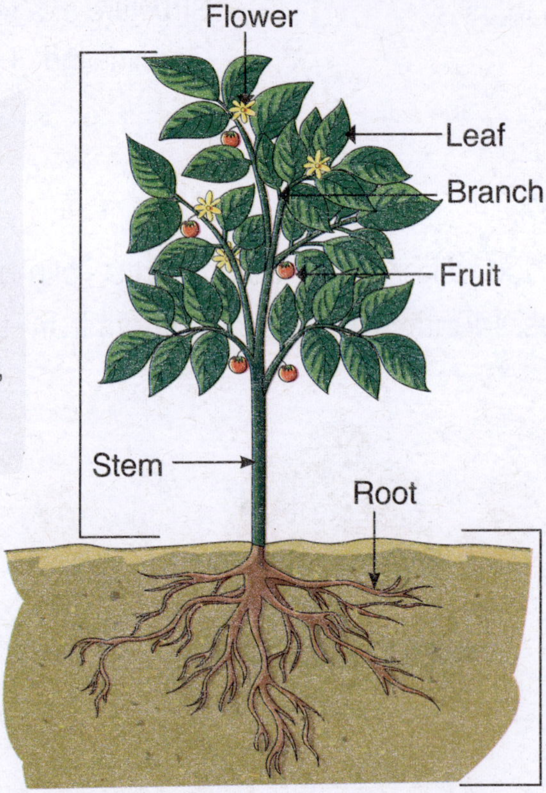

Parts of a plant

Root System:
The part of a plant that grows below the ground is called the root system. It consists of roots, which fix the plants to the soil.

ROOT SYSTEM

The root is the part of a plant that grows into the soil. There are two types of roots: **taproot** and **fibrous root**.

Taproot: It is the main root that grows from the end of a stem into the soil. A taproot has small, thin roots growing from its sides. Plants such as *Hibiscus*, radish and carrot have taproots.

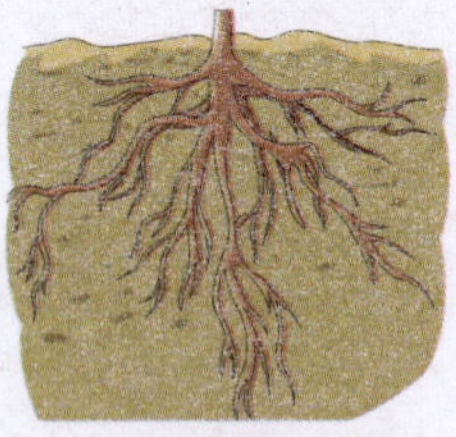

Taproot

Fibrous root: In some plants, there is no main root. Many fine roots grow directly from the end of the stem. Plants that have fibrous roots are grass, rice, wheat and onion.

Fibrous root

Functions of Roots

- Roots hold the plants firmly to the soil.
- Roots absorb water and minerals from the soil.
- Roots of some plants store extra food in them. Roots of plants such as radish, carrot and turnip are fleshy because they have food stored in them.

DO YOU KNOW?

Mangroves are trees that have roots growing above the soil.

SHOOT SYSTEM

The shoot is the part of a plant that grows above the soil. It consists of stems, leaves, flowers and fruits.

Stem

The stem is the main part of a plant. It grows above the soil and bears branches, leaves, flowers and fruits.

Different plants have different types of stems. The thick, woody stems of trees such as coconut, neem and mango are called **trunks**. A banana plant has a soft, green stem. Climbers and creepers such as grapevine and mint have weak stems that need support.

DO IT YOURSELF

Find out how plants drink water!

1. Fill a glass with water and add a few drops of red colour.
2. Take a white flower with a long stem and put it in the glass.

After some time, you will see a tinge of red in the white flower.

Do you know why?

The red-coloured water has travelled up the stem to reach the white flower.

Weak stems

Hard and woody stem

Functions of Stem

- The stem gives support to the plants and helps them to stand **upright**.
- The stem carries water from the roots to different parts of a plant.
- The stem carries food prepared by the leaves to different parts of a plant.
- The stem stores extra food prepared by the leaves. Plants such as sugarcane, ginger and potato store food in their stems.

WORD TO KNOW

upright: straight

Sugarcane

Ginger

QUICK REVISION

Give two examples for each of the following.

1. Plants with taproots __________ __________
2. Plants with fibrous roots __________ __________
3. Stems that store food __________ __________

The Leaf

Pick up a fallen leaf from the school garden and observe its different parts carefully.

- The structure that connects the stem to the leaves is called the **leaf stalk** or **petiole**.
- The thin tube running down the centre is called the **main vein**.
- The tubes coming out from the sides of the main vein are called **side veins**.
- The flat part of the leaf is called the **leaf blade** or **lamina**.

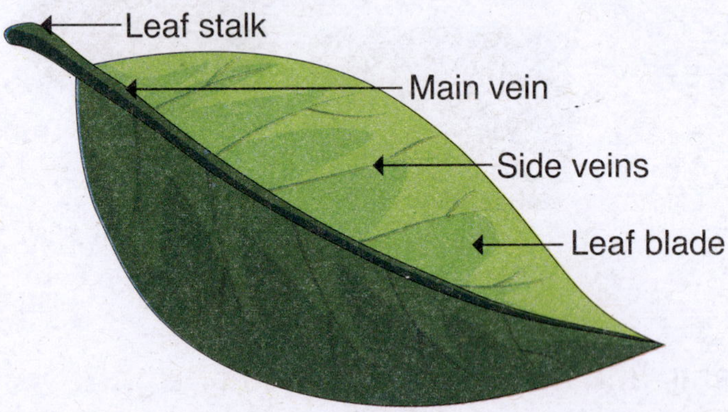

Parts of a leaf

The underside of leaves has tiny pores called **stomata**. Air enters and leaves a plant through these pores. Excess water in the plant gets released through these pores.

Leaves are green in colour due to the presence of a green substance called **chlorophyll**.

MEET LEAFY, THE COOK

She uses sunlight.

She uses water and minerals from the soil.

She uses carbon dioxide and chlorophyll.

Using these, she makes food for the plant.

The food she prepares is called sugar.

She stores the extra food as starch.

Functions of Leaves

- Leaves prepare food for the plant with the help of water, chlorophyll, sunlight and carbon dioxide. The process by which green plants make food is called **photosynthesis**.
- While making food for the plant, leaves give out oxygen that living things need to breathe.
- Leaves also store extra food. We eat leaves of some plants such as fenugreek, spinach and cabbage.

Fenugreek (methi) leaves

Spinach

Flowers

Flowers have different shapes, sizes and colours. Some flowers have **fragrance** while others do not. Most flowers grow into fruits.

> **WORD TO KNOW**
> fragrance: sweet smell

Flowers

Functions of Flowers

- Flowers make our surroundings fresh and beautiful.
- Flowers grow into fruits that carry seeds inside them. Seeds grow into new baby plants. Therefore, flowers help plants to reproduce.
- Flowers help to attract insects that suck nectar from them.

> **TALK TIME**
> Can you name these flowers?
>
> 
> ______________
>
> 
> ______________

Fruits

Most fruits have seeds inside them. New plants grow from these seeds. Some fruits have just one seed inside them, while some fruits have many seeds inside them.

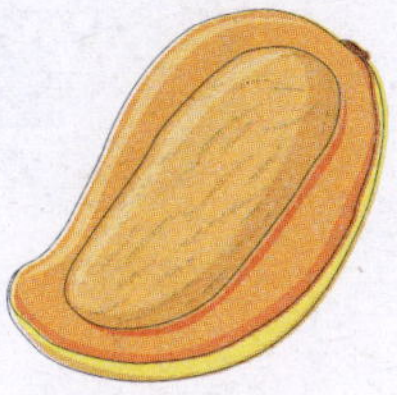
Mango with one seed

Watermelon with many seeds

We eat broccoli that is a flower! Can you name another flower that we eat?

DO IT YOURSELF

Make fruit salad using two one-seeded fruits and two many-seeded fruits. Remember to add a pinch of rock salt, a little sugar and a squeeze of lemon juice, and your fruit salad is ready.

SEEDS

Seeds grow into baby plants. The extra food stored in the seeds is used by the baby plant till it can make its food.

Let us learn about the structure of a seed, the types of seeds and how seeds produce a new plant.

Structure of a Seed

Look at the picture showing different parts of a seed. The outermost cover is called the **seed coat**, which protects the seed and the baby plant in it. The tiny hole in the seed coat is called the **micropyle**. Water is absorbed through the micropyle. Above the micropyle is a scar called **hilum**. It shows the place where the seed was attached to the fruit. The **embryo** is the baby plant that grows from the seed.

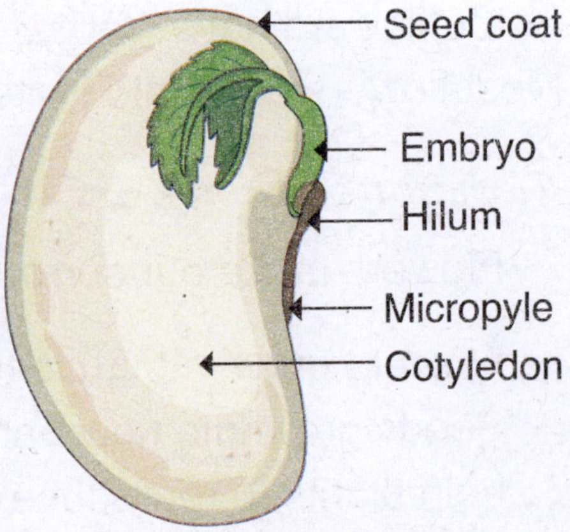

Parts of a seed

Types of Seeds

When we remove the seed coat, we see one or two fleshy white parts. These are called **seed leaves** or **cotyledons**.

Seeds such as peas, pulses and beans have two cotyledons and are called **dicotyledons** (di means two).

Seeds such as rice, wheat and maize have one cotyledon and are called **monocotyledons** (mono means one).

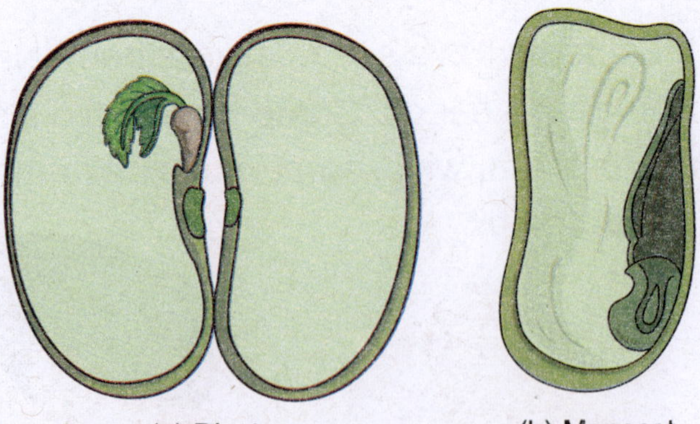

(a) Dicot (b) Monocot

Structure of a typical seed

Germination

The process of the growth of a seed into a new plant is called **germination**. Seeds grow into new plants when they get optimum **water**, **air** and **sunlight** and **soil**.

Name three oils that are made by crushing seeds of some plants. **FIND OUT**

Germination of a bean seed

DO IT YOURSELF

1. Fill an empty ice cream cup with soil.
2. Add some mustard seeds to the soil.
3. Sprinkle some water on the soil and keep the cup on the windowsill in sunlight.
4. Now, write your observations in the table below.

Day 1	Day 2	Day 3	Day 4	Day 5	Day 6

What do you think would have happened if you had not watered the seeds? Discuss your observations.

DO YOU KNOW?

We eat seeds such as rice, rajma, beans, peas and lentils. They are called **edible seeds.**

GREENATHON

- Why is our Earth called the Green Planet?
- Name two plants that grow in water.

CONCEPT MAP

Parts of a Plant

- **Root**

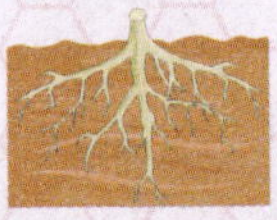

  - Holds the plant firmly to the soil
  - Absorbs water and minerals from the soil
  - Stores food
- **Stem**

  - Holds the plant upright
  - Carries food and water to different parts of the plant
  - Bears branches, leaves, flowers and fruits
- **Leaf**

  - Makes food for the plant
- **Flower**

  - Grows into a fruit
- **Fruit**

  - Has seeds inside it that grow into new plants

Seed

- Structure
  - Seed coat
  - Micropyle
  - Hilum
  - Cotyledons
  - Embryo
- Types
  - Monocotyledon
  - Dicotyledon

Things needed for germination of seeds

- Air
- Water
- Sunlight
- Soil

KEYWORDS

Root: the part of a plant that grows into the soil

Taproot: the main root that grows from the end of a stem into the soil

Fibrous root: many fine roots that grow from the end of the stem into the soil

Shoot: the part of a plant that grows above the soil

Photosynthesis: the process by which green plants make food

Germination: the process of the growth of a seed into a new plant

Cotyledons: seed leaves

Exercise

Objective Type Questions

A. Choose the correct answer.

1. Which of these plants has fibrous roots?
   a. Grass b. Carrot c. Radish d. Hibiscus
2. Which of these is a stem that we eat?
   a. Turnip b. Beetroot c. Potato d. Radish
3. Which of these are leaves that we eat?
   a. Broccoli b. Mushroom c. Cabbage d. Ginger
4. Flowers grow into which of the following?
   a. Buds b. Fruits c. Leaves d. Stems
5. Which of these is the flat part of a leaf?
   a. Lamina b. Petiole c. Main vein d. Side veins

B. Fill in the blanks.

1. The part of a plant that grows above the soil is called ______________ (root/shoot).
2. The part of a plant that grows into the soil is called ______________ (root/shoot).
3. Wheat has ______________ (tap/fibrous) roots.
4. The green colour of leaves is due to the presence of ______________ (stomata/chlorophyll).
5. ______________ (Photosynthesis/Respiration) is the process by which leaves make food for the plant.

C. Write T for True and F for False.

1. The stomata are found on the upper side of the leaf.
2. A banana plant has a trunk.
3. Leaves are green in colour due to the presence of stomata.
4. A watermelon has many seeds.
5. Peas have two cotyledons.

D. Name the following.

1. The thick woody stem of trees ______________
2. The part of the leaf that connects it to the stem ______________
3. The substance that provides green colour to leaves ______________
4. The outermost cover of a seed ______________
5. The baby plant that grows from a seed ______________

Subjective Type Questions

A. Define the following.

1. Shoot system
2. Lamina
3. Photosynthesis
4. Hilum
5. Cotyledon

B. Answer the following questions in brief.

1. Name the two types of roots. Give one example of each type.
2. Write two functions of roots.
3. Write two functions of stems.
4. How do plants make food?
5. Where does a plant store extra food?

C. Answer the following questions in detail.

1. What are the main parts of a plant? Explain.
2. Explain the different parts of a leaf.
3. Why are flowers important for plants?
4. What is germination? What does a seed need to germinate?
5. What are the two types of seeds? Give examples.

Application-based Questions

A. Plants take in carbon dioxide and give out oxygen during photosynthesis. What happens when they breathe during the day?

B. Anshul ate the seed of an apple by mistake. Her friend Abhijit says it will grow into a plant inside her. Do you think it is true? Why or why not?

Picture-based Questions

A. Label the parts of the plant in the picture given below.

B. Label the parts of the leaf given below.

Skill Booster

A. **21CS:** Creativity and Innovation, Communication | **CC:** English | **BT:** Cognitive, Psychomotor

Imagine yourself to be a plant/seed/tree/flower/fruit. What would your day be like? What would you see? What would you hear? Write a short story.

B. **21CS:** Initiative and Self-direction | **BT:** Psychomotor

Make a salad using different parts of a plant—leaf: lettuce; fruit: cucumber; root: carrot; seeds: peanuts; flower: broccoli (steamed); stem: potato (boiled).

Mix the above ingredients. Squeeze a lime and add salt, pepper and sugar or honey. Toss it and serve fresh. Garnish with chopped coriander leaves.

C. **21CS:** Critical Thinking | **CC:** General Knowledge | **BT:** Cognitive, Affective

Rani and her friends were playing in a garden. They were having a competition on who could pluck more leaves from trees. Do you think it was a good game? Talk about it in your class.

Worksheet 5

My SEE Journal

A. When you eat fruits at home, what can you do with the seeds instead of throwing them away?

B. If more fruit trees are planted in your neighbourhood, what changes can you expect to see in a few years?

My SDG Journal

15 LIFE ON LAND

A. What would the owner of the fruit farm do with the seeds?

B. How are the mango seeds different from the seeds of the melons?

C. Look up images of mango and melon plants on the Internet. What is the difference between these two types of plants?

6 Food We Get From Plants

Prior Knowledge

- Parts of a plant
- Things obtained from plants
- Edible parts of a plant

Learning Objectives

- Types of plants
- Parts of a plant used as a food
- How plants are useful to us

LET'S GET STARTED

We get food from both plants and animals. Circle the food products that are obtained from plants in the images given below:

1. 
Bread

2. 
Tomato soup

3. 
Omelette

4. 
Chicken

5. 
Chickpeas

6. 
Milk

When we look around, we see many types of plants. Some are tall such as a coconut tree, while some plants are short such as grass.

Plants are useful to us in many ways. They give us food to eat, oxygen to breathe and wood to make furniture. They hold the soil together, make the air pure and also give shade. Most importantly, they make the Earth green and beautiful. They are also homes to many animals and insects. In this chapter, let us learn about the different types of plants and the food that we get from them.

TYPES OF PLANTS

We have learned about different types of plants in previous classes. Let us revise.

Trees

Big and strong plants are called **trees**. They have thick woody stems known as **trunks**. They live for many years. Trees vary in shapes and sizes. For example, coconut tree, mango tree and neem tree.

A tree

Shrubs

Shrubs are small plants that have a bushy look. They have many woody stems and branches. For example, rose and *Hibiscus*.

Hibiscus

Rose

Herbs

Herbs are very small plants that have soft, thin and green stems. The stems are weak and break easily. Herbs live only for a season. For example, grass and mint.

Grass

Climbers

Plants with weak stems that need support (such as sticks, frames or walls) to grow straight are called **climbers**.

For example, money plant and grapevine.

Money plant

Creepers

Creepers are plants with weak stems that grow along the ground. For example, watermelon and pumpkin.

Pumpkin plant

PARTS OF PLANTS USED AS FOOD

Most of the food we eat come from plants. We eat different parts of plants.

We eat **leaves** of plants such as spinach, mint, cabbage and coriander.

We eat **roots** of plants such as carrots, beetroots, turnips and radish.

Cabbage

Spinach

Coriander

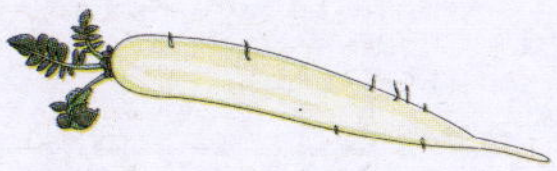

Radish

Turnip

Carrots

We eat **stems** of plants such as potato, ginger, sugarcane and yam.

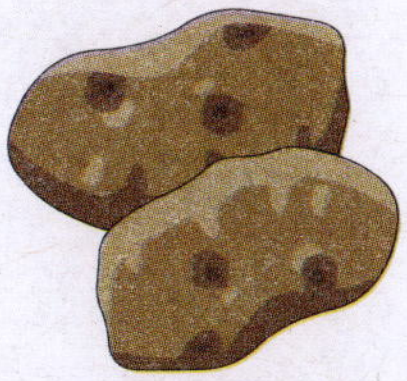

Potatoes

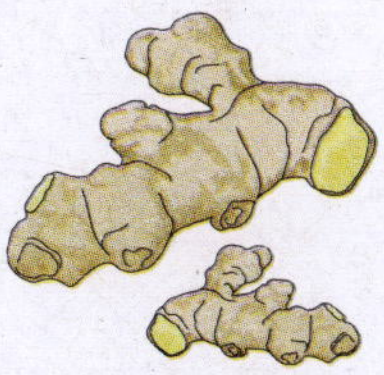

Ginger

Sugarcane

Cauliflower, clove and broccoli are some of the **flowers** that we eat.

Cauliflower

Broccoli

Name two food items that we make from the following food grains.

- Rice
- Wheat
- Corn

FIND OUT

We get cereals (food grains), pulses and oil from the **seeds** of some plants.

Some of the **cereals** are rice, wheat, jowar, bajra and corn.

Some examples of **pulses** are kidney beans (rajma), bengal gram (chana dal) and green gram (mung dal).

Green gram

Kidney beans

Urad dal

We get **oil** by crushing seeds of plants such as mustard, sesame (*til*), corn and groundnut. Some of the commonly used oils are groundnut oil, sunflower oil, olive oil, mustard oil and coconut oil.

Groundnut oil

Sunflower oil

Mustard oil

Here are some **fruits** that we eat.

Guava

Mango

Orange

Strawberry

Apple

QUICK REVISION

Name the following.

1. Thick woody stems of trees ____________
2. Very small plants with soft, thin, green stems ____________
3. Plants that need support to grow straight ____________
4. The plant part that gives us oil ____________

Other Food Items

Spices

We also get spices from plants. We add spices to our food to make the food tasty. Cardamom, cinnamon, pepper, cumin and cloves are some of the spices commonly used by us.

Cardamom

Pepper

Cloves

Nuts

We get nuts such as almonds, cashews, walnuts, hazelnuts and pistachio from plants.

Walnut

Cashew nuts

Almonds

DO YOU KNOW?

In Indian villages, people use neem twigs to brush their teeth as it helps them keep their teeth healthy and free from germs. The leaves and other parts of the neem tree are used to cure many diseases.

Medicines from Plants

Many medicines are made from plants such as *tulsi,* neem, mint, cloves and aloe vera.

Some seeds such as flax seeds, fenugreek (*methi*) and fennel seeds (*saunf*) are also used as medicines.

Mint leaves

Tea, Coffee and Cocoa from Plants

We get tea from tea leaves and coffee from coffee beans.

The cocoa that is used to make your favourite chocolates comes from the fruit of the cocoa tree.

Aloe vera

Cocoa plant

Cocoa beans

Chocolate

Sugar and Jaggery from Plants

Sugar and jaggery are made from sugarcane or sugarbeet.

Sugarcane

Jaggery

Sugar

CONCEPT MAP

Parts of a Plant That We Eat

Root	Stems	Leaves	Flower	Fruit	Seeds
Radish Carrot Beetroot Turnip	Potato Ginger Yam Sugarcane	Spinach Cabbage Lettuce Mint	Cauliflower Clove Broccoli	Apple Mango Papaya Orange	Nuts Cereals Spices Oil

KEYWORDS

Trees: big and strong plants

Shrubs: bushy plants with many stems

Herbs: plants with green stems that live for a season

Climbers: plants that need support for growing straight

Creepers: plants that grow along the ground

Cereals: food grains such as rice, wheat and bajra

Pulses: plant seeds that we eat

Spices: parts of a plant that we use to add flavour to food

Exercise

Objective Type Questions

A. Choose the correct option.

1. ______________ is a vegetable.
   a. Mango b. Coconut c. Cabbage d. Wheat
2. ______________ is not the seed of a plant.
   a. Spinach b. Groundnut c. Cashew nut d. Rice
3. ______________ is prepared using wheat.
   a. Rice flakes b. Roti c. Fried rice d. Oil
4. Which of the following does not give oil?
   a. Coconut b. Mustard c. Carrot d. Groundnut
5. Which of these is a spice?
   a. Rajma b. Rice c. Clove d. Wheat

B. Fill in the blanks.

1. We get jaggery from ______________ plant. (sugarcane/rose)
2. We make medicines from ______________. (mint/rice)
3. Rice is the ______________ of a plant. (cereal/stem)
4. Ginger is a ______________. (root/stem)
5. We make noodles from ______________. (wheat/pulses)

C. Circle the odd one out.

1. Rice, dal, wheat, clove
2. Mustard, orange, sunflower, olive
3. Clove, dal, cardamom, pepper
4. Potato, ginger, brinjal, sugarcane
5. Mango, carrot, orange, apple

D. Give two examples for each of the following we eat.

1. Roots ______________ ______________
2. Stem ______________ ______________
3. Leaves ______________ ______________
4. Flower ______________ ______________
5. Seeds ______________ ______________

Subjective Type Questions

A. Answer the following in brief.

1. List the seeds from which we get oil for cooking.
2. Name three seeds we use as spices to flavour our food.
3. Which part of the plant is used to make coffee and chocolate?
4. Name some food items made from wheat.
5. Name some nuts we obtain from plants.

B. Answer the following questions in detail.

1. List the different types of plants. Give two examples of each.
2. How do we get oil from plants?
3. Draw and name one of each that we eat: stem, root, leaf, seed, flower, fruit.
4. How do we obtain medicines from plants?

Application-based Question

How is mustard oil different from rice bran oil?

Picture-based Question

Identify the parts of the plants we eat from the pictures given below.

__________ __________ __________ __________ __________

Skill Booster

A. 21CS: Information Literacy | EL | BT: Cognitive, Psychomotor

Visit a nearby store and collect the following data:

1. Names of four products made from wheat
2. Names of five kinds of spices used for cooking
3. Names of five dals we eat

Put up your list on the board and compare your list with your classmates.

B. 21CS: Information Literacy | CC: English | BT: Cognitive

English has several idioms and phrases with fruits/vegetables. Some of these are given below. Can you add to the list?

Also, find out their meaning.

1. An apple a day keeps the doctor away.
2. Apple of my eye
3. Two peas in a pod
4. ______________________________
5. ______________________________

Worksheet 6

My SEE Journal

A. Apart from its fruit, what other parts of the banana plant are eaten?

____

____

____

____

____

B. What are the leaves of the banana plant used for?

____

____

____

____

____

____

My SDG Journal

12 RESPONSIBLE CONSUMPTION AND PRODUCTION

A. Why are plants so important to us?

____

____

____

____

____

B. Do you have plants at home? Adopt a plant today. How will you take care of it?

____

____

____

____

____

7 Forms of Matter: Solids, Liquids and Gases

Prior Knowledge

- Things around us exist as solid, liquid or gas.
- Water is liquid, ice is solid and water vapour is gas.

Learning Objectives

- What is matter?
- Properties of solids, liquids and gases
- Change of forms
- Uses of matter

LET'S GET STARTED

Look at the pictures given below and write S for solid, L for liquid and G for gas.

1

Water

○

2

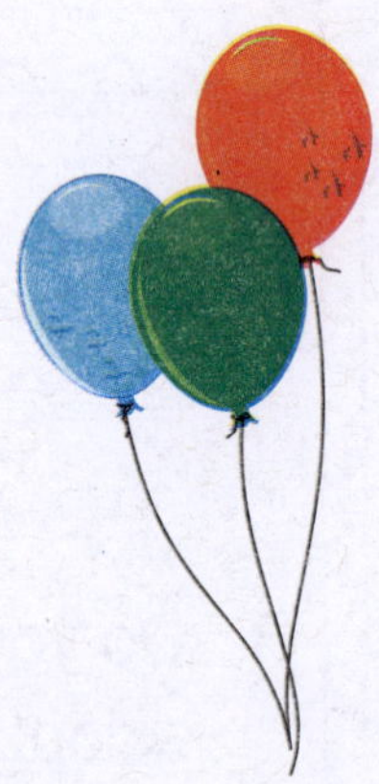

Air in balloons

○

3

Book

○

Look around the classroom and name any ten things that you see, such as people, books and board. Do these all look alike? No, they have different shapes, colours and sizes.

MATTER

Anything around us which has mass and occupies space is called **matter**. Mass shows us how heavy or light an object is.

Which of these has more mass?

A feather or a notebook? An elephant or a monkey?

Matter exists in three different forms—solid, liquid and gas.

Solids

Look carefully at a book. What is its shape? How much space does it occupy? Does it change its shape or occupy less/more space when you put it somewhere else?

> **TALK TIME**
>
> Pick up any two objects in your classroom. Now, discuss how these are similar as well as different from each other.

A book is an example of a solid. It does not change its shape or occupy more space when it is put on a shelf or in a bag.

A solid is hard. It has a **definite** shape and size, and it occupies a definite space. Solids cannot flow easily on their own. A bottle, watch and rock are examples of solids.

> **WORD TO KNOW**
>
> definite: fixed

Can you name five solid objects that you see in your school?

Eraser

Pencil

Book

Blackboard

Liquids

Take some fruit juice in a glass. Now, pour it into a bowl. Does it change shape? What do you think will happen if you pour the juice onto a table?

The juice is an example of a liquid. A liquid has no shape or size of its own. It takes the shape of the container it is poured into. However, a liquid occupies a definite space. The container it is poured into may be big or small, but the space it occupies remains the same. Liquids can flow easily. Juice, oil, milk and honey are examples of liquids.

Juice

Oil

Milk

Gases

Balloons filled with air

A football filled with air

Blow air into a balloon. What happens to the balloon? Now, release the air inside it. What happens to the balloon when the air inside it is released?

The air that we blow into the balloon is a mixture of gases. Like liquids, gases also do not have a definite shape or size. They flow easily in all directions. This is the reason we can smell perfume, which is a gas, even from afar.

Air and water vapour (steam) are examples of gases.

QUICK REVISION

Write T for True and F for False.

1. Matter exists in two forms.
2. Solids do not have a definite shape.
3. Liquids take the shape of the container they are poured into.
4. Steam is an example of gas.

Change of Forms

DO IT YOURSELF

Light a candle with the help of an elder. Notice how the solid wax melts into a liquid state. Then, cool it. What do you see?

What happens to an ice cream if you take it out of the freezer and keep it outside for ten minutes?

It melts. What do you do to make it solid again? You put it back in the freezer.

This shows that some things can change their forms easily without losing their properties.

Do you think the same thing will happen if we keep a rubber ball in a freezer and leave it outside after that?

Water, as you have learned in Class 2, exists in three forms—solid (ice), liquid (water) and gas (water vapour).

The forms of water change upon heating or cooling.

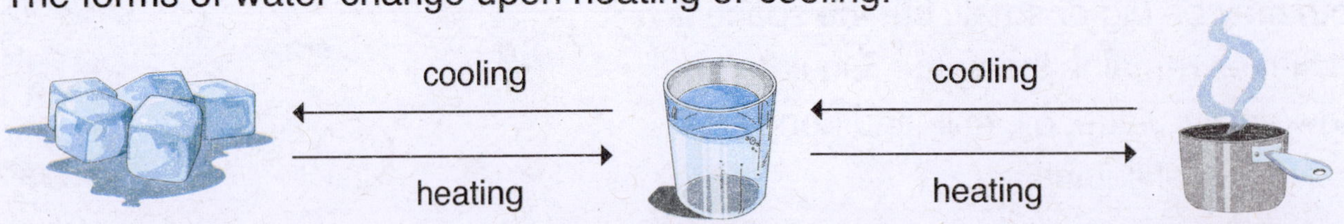

Ice *Water* *Water vapour*

- A solid changes into liquid on heating. This process is called **melting**. For example, ice melts to form water.
- A liquid changes into solid on cooling. This process is called **freezing**. For example, water freezes to form ice.
- A liquid changes into gas on heating. This process is called **evaporation**. For example, water evaporates to form steam or water vapour.
- A gas changes into liquid on cooling. This process is called **condensation**. For example, water vapour in the air condenses to form droplets on a cool surface.

DO IT YOURSELF

1. Take a glass and fill it up with water or any other liquid of your choice.
2. Add a few ice cubes to it and keep it aside for five minutes.
3. After some time, you will see tiny water droplets on the outer surface of the glass.

This happens because the water vapour in the air around the glass condenses as soon as it comes in contact with the cool outer surface of the glass. The condensed water vapour appears in the form of tiny water droplets.

Uses of Matter

Everything around us is made up of matter. The food we eat, the air we breathe, the water we drink, the clothes we wear, the books we read, the toys we play with, the plants and animals around us and even our own body is made of matter.

DO YOU KNOW?

Some solid substances such as camphor and naphthalene balls change directly into the gaseous state.

Everything around us is made up of matter.

CONCEPT MAP

Matter

↓

Three States

Solid

- Definite shape
- Occupies definite space
- Does not flow

Liquid

- No definite shape
- Occupies definite space
- Can flow

Gas

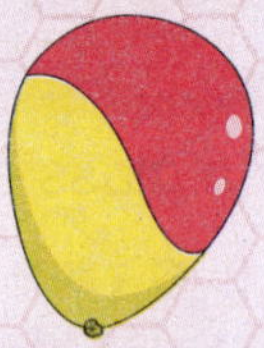

- No definite shape
- Occupies no definite space
- Flows freely in all directions

KEYWORDS

Matter: anything that has mass and occupies space

Mass: shows how heavy or light an object is

Solid: the form of matter that has a definite shape and size and occupies a definite space

Liquid: the form of matter that has no definite shape but occupies a definite space

Gas: the form of matter that has no definite shape or size and flows easily in all directions

Melting: change of a solid into a liquid on heating

Evaporation: change of a liquid into a gas on heating

Condensation: change of a gas into a liquid on cooling

Freezing: change of a liquid into a solid on cooling

Exercise

Objective Type Questions

A. Choose the correct answer.

1. Which one of these is not a solid?
   a. Dust b. Rock c. Honey d. Pencil
2. Which of these does not take the shape of the container it is kept in?
   a. Milk b. Soup c. Bread d. Lemonade
3. What would you do to change a solid into a liquid?
   a. Heat it b. Cool it c. Bend it d. Store it
4. When water vapour is condensed, what does it turn into?
   a. Water droplets b. Gas c. Ice d. Steam
5. Which of the following flows freely in all directions?
   a. Water b. Soil c. Cereals d. Air

B. Fill in the blanks.

1. Matter has ______________ (mass/life) and occupies ______________. (length/space)
2. ______________ (Solids/Liquids) have a definite shape and size.
3. An example of a gas is ______________. (steam/onion)
4. The process of water changing into ice is called ______________. (condensation/freezing)
5. The process of solid wax changing into liquid on heating is called ______________. (evaporation/melting)

C. Match the following.

1. Evaporation	a. Water drops on a cold drink bottle
2. Condensation	b. Water changing to water vapour
3. Freezing	c. Ice changing to water
4. Melting	d. Water changing to ice

D. Write T for True and F for False.

1. Liquids can flow easily.
2. Milk has a definite shape.
3. Air easily flows in all directions.
4. Water vapour is an example of a liquid.
5. Change in the form of a matter happens only on heating.

Subjective Type Questions

A. Answer the following questions in brief.

1. What is matter? Give two examples.
2. What are the three forms of matter?
3. Write two properties of solids.

4. Write two properties of liquids.
5. What is melting?

B. Answer the following questions in detail.

1. List some characteristics of solids.
2. How are liquids different from gases?
3. What is meant by evaporation and condensation?
4. How does water change its form?

Application-based Questions

A. When you spray room freshener, its fragrance spreads very quickly. Why?

B. What happens to the soaked water when you hang your wet clothes in the sun?

Picture-based Question

Name the processes that change the forms of water in the following examples.

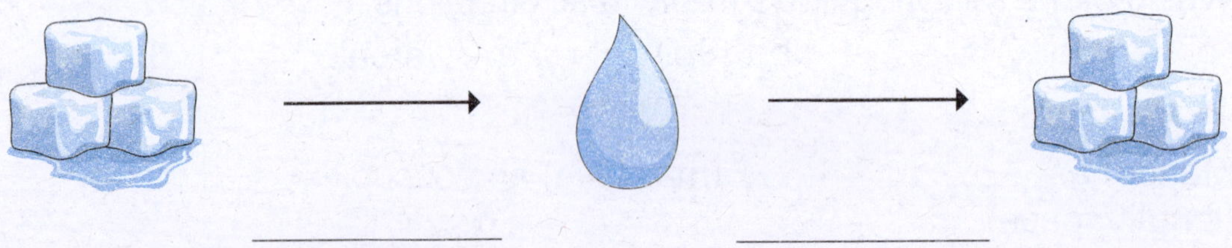

Skill Booster

A. 21CS: Creativity and Innovation | EL | BT: Psychomotor

Science in the kitchen

Put on your chef's hat and see the change in the state of matter.

You will need:

- a large, deep bowl
- a packet of jelly crystals
- 1 ½ cups of hot water
- 1 ½ cups of cold water

Method:

1. Put the jelly crystals in the bowl.
2. Add boiling-hot water and stir well, making sure all the jelly crystals get dissolved.
3. Add cold water and stir again.
4. Put the bowl in the refrigerator for 3–4 hours.

Surprise everybody by showing how the crystals and water changed their forms!

B. 21CS: Information Literacy | CC: Social Studies | BT: Cognitive

Hazel's family is making holiday plans to visit an ice museum. These museums have statues made of ice. The family has to choose among Alaska, Norway, Switzerland and Dubai. Use your atlas to find the location of these places. Find out which place will be closest to India.

Worksheet 7

My SEE Journal

A. Rishabh is helping his mother dry clothes. What quality does this show about Rishabh?

B. Do you help your parents in their routine tasks at home? What do you do to share their work?

My SDG Journal

4 QUALITY EDUCATION

A. How do clothes dry while hanging on a line?

B. On which days will clothes dry faster—sunny, cloudy or windy?

C. How is the process of drying of clothes in the sun different from boiling of water?

8 Some Properties of Water

Prior Knowledge

- Sources of water
- Uses of water
- Need to save water

Learning Objectives

- Physical properties of water
- Objects that float and sink in water

LET'S GET STARTED

We use water for various activities in our everyday life. Draw and write any two uses of water in the space given below.

1

___

___

2

___

___

Water has certain properties that make it a very useful substance for us. In this chapter, we will learn about these properties through some activities.

PHYSICAL PROPERTIES OF WATER

- Take some drinking water in a glass tumbler and keep it in front of you.

  What colour is it?

  Now, smell it. What does it smell of?

  Take a sip of water. What does it taste like?

  What can you say about water based on your observations?

  Pure water, as you know, has **no colour**, **taste** or **smell**.

- Water has **no shape** of its own. It takes the shape of the container into which it is poured.

- Water **occupies space**.

  If you pour water into an empty glass, you will see it occupies the space inside the glass. Now, if you pour water from that glass into a bottle, you will see that there also, the water takes up some space. This shows water occupies space.

- Many **things dissolve** (completely mix) in water.

- **Water exists in three states of matter: water as liquid, ice as solid and water vapour or steam as gas.**

DO IT YOURSELF

1. Place three different types of containers in front of you: a bottle, a bowl and a glass.
2. Take a cup of water.
3. Pour the water into different containers. What do you see?

You will see the water takes the shape of the container into which it is poured. Now, pour the water back into the cup.

Do you see any change in the amount of water that was there at the beginning of the experiment? (Yes/No)

This shows that the shape of water changes but the total amount of water remains the same!

Water can change its form upon cooling or heating.

Conversion among three states of water

WATER AND WATER SOLUTIONS

Some solids dissolve (completely mix) in liquids. The solid that dissolves in a liquid is called the **solute**. The liquid in which the solute dissolves is called the **solvent**. The liquid formed after dissolving a solute in a solvent is called a **solution**.

DO IT YOURSELF

1. Take a glassful of drinking water in a vessel. Add a teaspoon of salt to the water.
2. Stir the water well. What happens to the salt after some time?
3. Now, taste the water from the vessel. Do you find any change in the taste?

Water in the vessel tastes salty.

This happens because salt dissolves in water.

When we dissolve something in water, we get a **water solution**. For example, as you have learned from the Do It Yourself activity given above, when we stir salt or sugar in water, we get a salt or sugar solution.

DO YOU KNOW?

Water dissolves almost everything. Hence, it is called a **universal solvent**.

Conditions That Affect the Making of a Solution

Some conditions that affect the making of a solution are given below:

- **Stirring:** Stirring the water helps the solute particles to dissolve faster.
- **Temperature of the water:** Solute particles dissolve faster in warm water. Therefore, heating the water helps the solute to dissolve faster.

DO IT YOURSELF

1. Take a glass of warm water and another glass with cold water.
2. Take the items mentioned in the table and try dissolving each of them in the glasses one by one.
3. Keep a note of your observations in the table given below:

Item	Not Stirring	Stirring	Cold Water	Warm Water	Your Observations
Food colour or ink					
Sugar					
Sand					

QUICK REVISION

Write T for True and F for False.

1. Water has a taste of its own.
2. If water is poured into a glass, it takes the shape of the glass.
3. Water flows easily.
4. In a salt solution, we can see the solute.

Floating and Sinking

Some objects float in water (for example, a paper boat or a piece of cork), while some objects sink (for example, an iron nail or a steel spoon).

(a)

(b)

A paper boat floats on water but an iron nail sinks in water.

Let us do an activity to find out what floats and what sinks in water.

1. Take the items listed in the table below and predict which objects will float and which ones will sink.
2. Then, drop these objects one by one in a bucket of water and check whether your predictions were correct.

Record your observations in the table given below.

Items	Will the object float or sink in water? (Prediction)	Does the object float or sink in water? (Observation)
Potato		
Onion		
Lemon		
Coin		
Feather		
Stone		
Coconut		
A twig		
Empty plastic bottle		
Spoon		
Rubber duck		

CONCEPT MAP

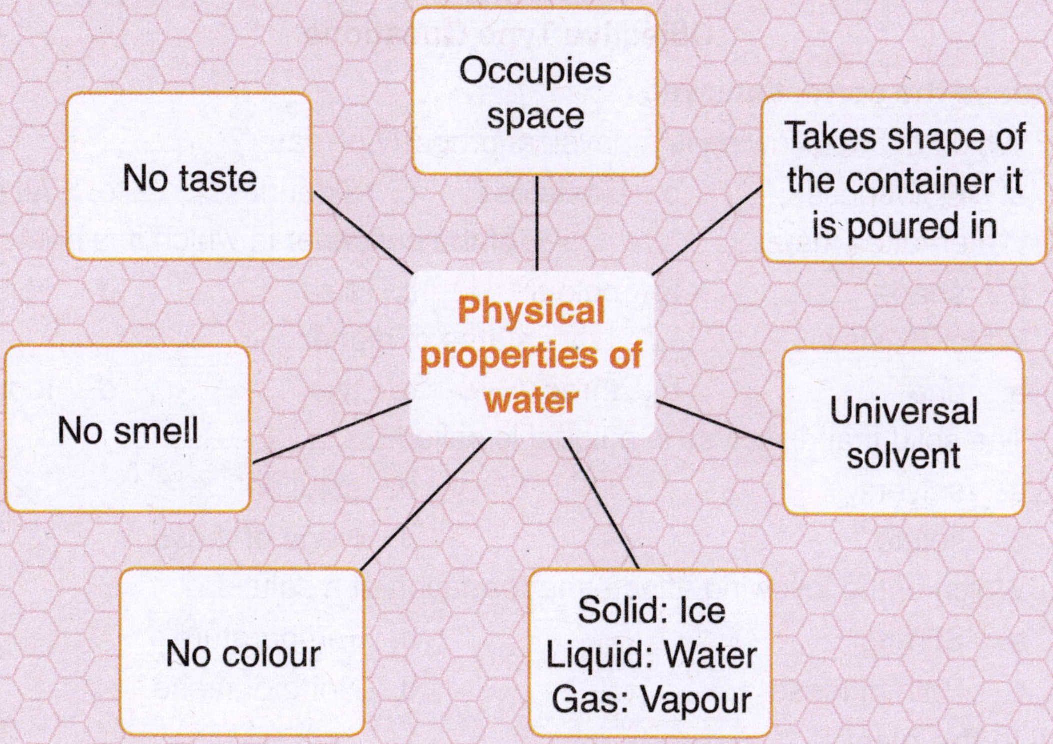

KEYWORDS

Solute: the solid that dissolves in a liquid

Solvent: the liquid in which the solute dissolves

Solution: the liquid obtained after dissolving a solute in a solvent

Water solution: the solution obtained when something is dissolved in water

Exercise

Objective Type Questions

A. Choose the correct answer.

1. Which of the following is a physical property of water?
   a. Colourless b. Tasteless c. Odourless d. All of these
2. Water takes the ______________ of the container in which it is poured in.
   a. shape b. colour c. size d. volume
3. Water exists in ______________ states of matter.
   a. one b. three c. two d. four
4. The solid that dissolves in a liquid is called ______________.
   a. solvent b. solution
   c. solute d. None of these
5. Which of the following affects the formation of a solution?
   a. Stirring b. Temperature
   c. Both of these d. None of these

B. Fill in the blanks.

1. ______________ is a universal solvent. (Water/Milk)
2. Pure water has no colour, taste or ______________. (state/smell)
3. The liquid in which the solute dissolves is called a ______________. (solution/solvent)
4. Pumice stone ______________ in water. (floats/sinks)

C. Write T for True and F for False.

1. When poured into a jug, water takes the shape of the jug.
2. Sugar dissolves in water.
3. Water does not change its form.
4. A solute dissolves faster in a cold solvent.
5. A key sinks in water.

Subjective Type Questions

A. Define the following.

1. Solute 2. Solvent 3. Solution

B. Answer the following questions in brief.

1. List any two physical properties of water.
2. What are the three states of water? How can it be converted from one state to another?

3. How can we prepare a water solution?
4. Name two objects that float in water and two objects that sink.

C. Answer the following questions in detail.

1. Write a note on water solution.
2. How can we increase the ability of water to dissolve a solute?

Application-based Question

Why does a ship float in water but an iron nail sinks?

Picture-based Questions

A. Put a tick mark for the objects that will float on water and a cross mark for the objects that will sink.

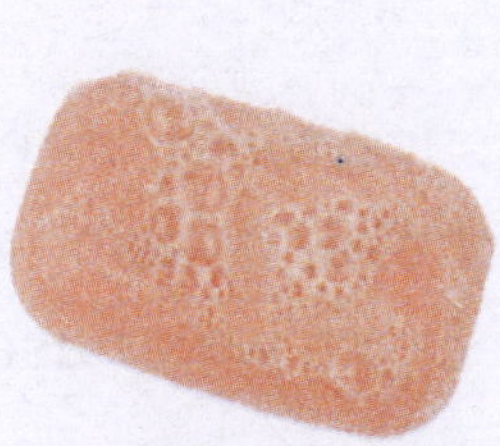

Soap

Leaf

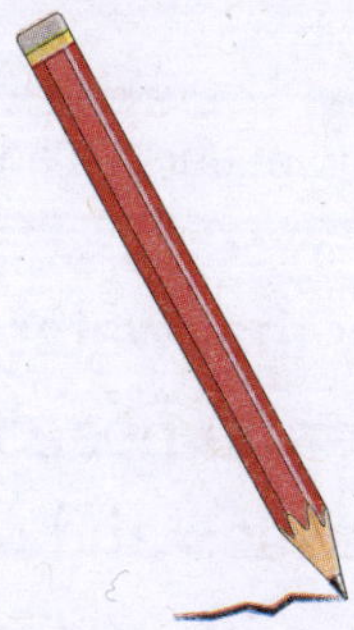

Pencil

B. Tick the objects that will dissolve in water.

Toothpaste

Egg shell

Sugar

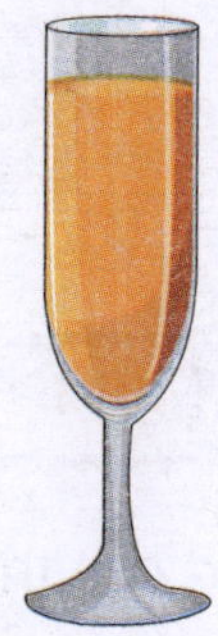

Orange juice

Honey

Cloves

Coconut oil

Detergent powder

Skill Booster

A. 21CS: Creativity and Innovation, Collaboration | EL | BT: Cognitive, Psychomotor

Form groups of five. Each one should bring one edible item from home, such as salt, sugar, lime juice, orange squash, rose syrup and honey, that dissolves in water. Do not show it to each other. Now, one of you will be blindfolded and one of the others will mix their ingredient in a glass of drinking water. The blindfolded person has to taste the solution and guess what has been dissolved.

B. 21CS: Leadership and Responsibility | BT: Cognitive, Affective

We know that water is a precious resource. So, we should save water or reuse it for other purposes. At our homes, we should collect the leftover drinking water in our glasses and use it to water plants. We may also collect the water used for washing fruits and vegetables to water our plants.

Can you think of two more ways to reuse water?

____

____

C. 21CS: Information Literacy | CC: English | BT: Cognitive

Find out the meaning of the water sounds given below and make sentences using them. Also, add two more to the list.

Gurgling: ______________________________

Pitter-patter: ______________________________

Splash: ______________________________

__________: ______________________________

__________: ______________________________

Worksheet 8

My SEE Journal

A. Swati accepted her mistake. Her mother also did not scold her. What qualities does this show of them?

____

____

____

____

B. What do you do when you make a mistake?

____

____

____

____

____

My SDG Journal

4 QUALITY EDUCATION

A. How would Swati's mother remove the salt from the rice?

____

____

____

____

____

____

B. Is there another way by which the salt can be removed from the rice?

____

____

____

____

9 Water as a Resource

Prior Knowledge

- Three forms of water
- Sources of water
- Physical properties of water

Learning Objectives

- Change of states of water
- Water cycle
- Impurities in water
- Purification of water
- Rainwater harvesting

LET'S GET STARTED

You already know water exists in three forms. Fill in the blanks by taking hints from the pictures given below to name the three forms of water.

1. Abhishek is drinking ________ from the bottle.
2. ________ is coming out from the boiling water in the pan.
3. Kriti is taking out ________ cubes from the tray.

DO IT YOURSELF

1. Put four cubes of ice on a plate and leave them outside for a while. What happens to them?
2. Collect the water in a kettle and take an elder's help to heat it till it boils. What do you see?
3. Hold a cold metal plate in front of the spout. Now, what do you see?

You will see that the ice (water in solid form) melts into water (liquid form), which on heating becomes steam.

When steam is cooled, it becomes water again, which on freezing changes to form ice.

Thus, we see that water exists in three forms.

WATER

All living things need water to live.

Water is needed for drinking, washing, cleaning and cooking.

FIND OUT: How do plants get their supply of water?

States of Water

In Chapter 8, you learnt that water exists in three forms: in liquid form as water, in solid form as ice and in gaseous form as water vapour. Water can be converted from one state to another upon heating or cooling.

(a) Solid: ice (b) Liquid: water (c) Gas: water vapour

Three forms of water

DO IT YOURSELF

Try the following activities:

A. Watch your mother boil some water in an open pan. What do you see?

You see steam coming out once the water starts boiling. The heat changes the water into water vapour or steam, which then merges with air.

B. Put some ice cubes in a glass of water for a few minutes. What do you see on the outer surface of the glass?

You see that droplets of water have formed on the outer surface of the glass. These droplets form when the water vapour in the air comes in contact with the cold surface of the glass and turns into water again.

WATER CYCLE

In nature, there is a continuous cycle in which water keeps changing its form. This is called the **water cycle**.

The heat of the sun warms up the water in rivers, lakes, oceans and other waterbodies. This water turns into water vapour. This process is called **evaporation**.

Water vapour is light, so it rises up (just like a gas balloon). As it moves up, it comes in contact with cool air and changes into tiny droplets of water. This is called **condensation**.

These tiny water droplets join together to form clouds.

When the clouds become too heavy, the water falls down as rain. This is called **precipitation**.

Water cycle

Once again, rainwater fills the waterbodies and some of it seeps underground. The continuous cycle in which water changes from water vapour to liquid water through condensation and precipitation and then back to water vapour through evaporation is called **water cycle**.

QUICK REVISION

Explain the following terms with respect to the water cycle.

1. Evaporation: ____________________
2. Condensation: ____________________
3. Precipitation: ____________________

WHAT MAKES WATER DIRTY OR IMPURE?

Rainwater is the purest form of natural water. However, before it reaches the Earth, certain impurities get mixed with it. The following impurities make water dirty:

- Dust particles
- Mud and sand
- Gases
- Germs

TALK TIME

Collect a glass of water from a puddle and observe all the impurities in it. Can you name them?

PURIFICATION OF WATER

Sometimes, water that looks clear may contain germs and other dissolved impurities.

> **DO YOU KNOW?**
> The drinking water that reaches our home is cleaned in the city's water works to remove all germs and dirt.

Impurities that dissolve in water and are invisible are called **soluble impurities**, for example, salt. On the other hand, impurities that are not soluble in water and can be easily seen are called **insoluble impurities**, for example, sand. To stay healthy, we must drink water that has been purified. Drinking dirty water may cause diseases such as cholera, typhoid and diarrhoea.

Removing Insoluble Impurities

Filtration

Filtration is a process in which insoluble impurities are separated by passing water through filters. Usually, a filter paper is folded in the shape of a cone and fitted in a funnel through which water is passed. It holds back the solid impurities and allows the clean water to pass through.

Filtration

Sedimentation and Decantation

In this method, water is kept undisturbed for some time. The heavy impurities settle down at the bottom of the container leaving the clear water on top. This process is called **sedimentation**.

The clear water on top is slowly poured into another container. This is called **decantation**.

Sedimentation *Decantation*

Removing Soluble Impurities

Boiling

The easiest way to purify water is to boil it for 10–15 minutes. This kills the germs present in water.

Boiling

Chlorination

Chlorination is the addition of chlorine gas or chlorine tablets to water to kill germs and make water fit for drinking.

Purifying Water at Home

We can remove the impurities in water at home by the following methods:

- straining water (using a strainer, fine cloth or fine mesh)
- by boiling water
- using water purifiers
- using chlorine (a chemical) to kill germs in water

DO IT YOURSELF

1. Take some water in a jug and mix some sand in it to make sandy water.
2. Now, take a jug made of glass and tie a thin cloth around the mouth of the jug.
3. Now, pour the sandy water through the cloth into the glass jug.

You will see that the sand stays behind in the cloth, while the clean water is collected in the glass jug.

RAINWATER HARVESTING

Rainwater harvesting is a way of collecting rainwater from surfaces on which rain falls, filtering it and storing it for different uses.

Rainwater may be collected from roofs of buildings and then stored inside a special tank. It may also be collected in barrels and drums.

Rainwater harvesting helps us to reuse water for many purposes such as watering plants in the garden or washing clothes and dishes. It also helps in reducing soil erosion.

Collecting rainwater in a ground-level tank

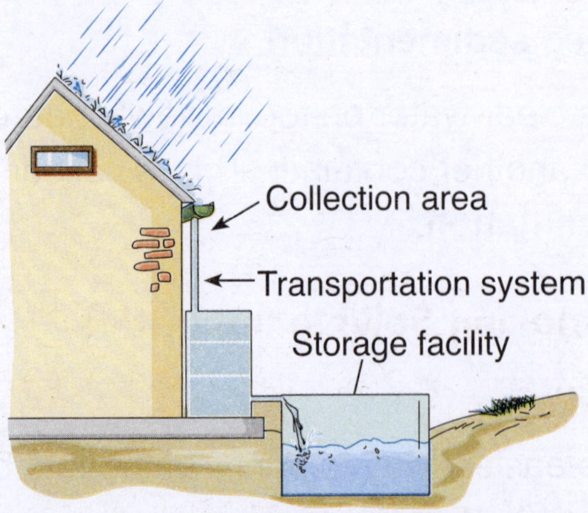

Collecting rainwater underground

CONCEPT MAP

Processes Involved in Water Cycle

- Evaporation
- Condensation
- Precipitation

Impurities in Water

- Dust
- Mud
- Sand
- Gases
- Germs

KEYWORDS

Evaporation: changing of water into water vapour upon warming

Condensation: changing of water vapour into droplets of water upon cooling

Precipitation: the falling of rain or snow

Water cycle: the continuous cycle in which water changes from water vapour to liquid water through condensation and precipitation and then back to water vapour through evaporation

Filtration: the process in which insoluble impurities are separated by passing the water through filters

Sedimentation: the process of settling down impurities at the bottom of a container to form clear water at the top

Decantation: the process of pouring the clear water collected at the top of a container into another container

Chlorination: the addition of chlorine gas or tablets to water to kill the germs present in it

Rainwater harvesting: the process of collecting rainwater from surfaces on which rain falls, filtering it and storing it for different uses

Exercise

Objective Type Questions

A. Choose the correct answer.

1. Water exists in ______________ forms in nature.

   a. two b. three c. four d. five

2. The conversion of water vapour into water upon cooling is called ______________.

   a. precipitation b. evaporation c. condensation d. melting

3. The falling of rain from clouds is called ______________.

   a. precipitation b. evaporation c. condensation d. freezing

4. To remove soluble impurities from water, we use the process of ______________.

   a. boiling b. filtration c. sedimentation d. decantation

B. Fill in the blanks.

1. The state of water may be changed by ______________ (filtering/heating) or ______________ (cooling/straining).
2. ______________ (Rainwater/Sea water) is the purest form of water.
3. ______________ (Chlorine/Fluorine) is a chemical used to kill germs in water.
4. Rainwater helps to prevent ______________ (wind/soil) erosion.
5. When water ______________ (drops/vapours) become too heavy, they fall as rain.

C. Write T for True and F for False.

1. Steam is the liquid form of water.
2. Rainwater may be collected underground too.
3. Water cannot have gases dissolved in them.
4. The conversion of water into water vapour is called evaporation.

Subjective Type Questions

A. Define the following.

1. Filtration
2. Sedimentation
3. Decantation
4. Chlorination

B. Answer the following questions in brief.

1. Name the three states of water.
2. What makes water impure?
3. What is water cycle?
4. Write two forms of precipitation.
5. Define evaporation.

C. Answer the following questions in detail.

1. Explain the different ways in which water can be purified at home.
2. Describe the water cycle in nature. Draw and label.
3. How is evaporation different from condensation?
4. What is rainwater harvesting? How is it useful?
5. How do you collect and store rainwater?

Application-based Question

What happens to the puddles of water formed on the ground once the rain stops? Why?

Picture-based Question

Identify the different ways to remove impurities from water shown in the images below.

______________ ______________ ______________ ______________

Skill Booster

A. 21CS: Creativity and Innovation | EL | BT: Cognitive, Psychomotor

Ask an elder to heat some water till it starts forming steam and then pour the water into a glass jar. Cover the jar with a plate and wait for a few minutes. Put some ice cubes on top of the plate and watch closely to see what happens inside the jar. Water drops will begin to fall like rain from the plate!

The cold surface of the plate because of the ice cubes kept on it cools the steam, changing it back to water, which falls like raindrops.

B. 21CS: Critical Thinking | BT: Cognitive, Affective

A washing machine uses a lot of water to wash clothes and a dryer takes a lot of electricity to dry clothes. Which is a better option that can save both water and electricity?

Tick the correct statement.

1. Handwash clothes and dry them in the dryer.
2. Handwash clothes and dry them in the sun.

Worksheet 9

My SEE Journal

A. Where did the water in the stream come from?

____

____

____

B. Why is the water of the stream so cold?

____

____

____

C. Why is the water of the stream so pure?

____

____

____

____

My SDG Journal

6 CLEAN WATER AND SANITATION

A. Where does the Ganges river get its water from?

____

____

____

____

____

B. Why is the water in the Ganges not as pure as the mountain stream?

____

____

____

____

____

10 Sun as a Natural Resource

Prior Knowledge

- Sun as a star
- Solar system
- Heat and light energy from the sun

Learning Objectives

- Sun as a natural source of energy
- Renewable and non-renewable sources of energy
- Conservation of energy

LET'S GET STARTED

Have you ever imagined how life would be if the sun decides to go on a holiday? Discuss this in class, and write any three ways in which this could affect your life.

1. ______________________
2. ______________________
3. ______________________

Sun is the source of heat and light energy on Earth.

ENERGY FROM SUN

Sun is the Earth's most important source of energy. The word 'solar' means 'from the sun'. So, solar energy means energy from the sun.

> **DO YOU KNOW?**
>
> Sunlight is a source of Vitamin D.
>
> 

Light is a form of energy that helps us to see. During the day, the sun helps us see things around us. At night, the light from the moon enables us to see the surroundings. Remember, the moon has no light of its own. It reflects the light of the sun. Thus, directly or indirectly, the sun is the main natural source of light energy on Earth. Besides, sunlight is also needed by plants to make food through the process of photosynthesis.

The sun also provides us with heat energy. The heat from the sun helps us to stay warm. Without the heat energy from the sun, the Earth would be too cold for living things to survive. Plants would not grow, and there would be no food for animals. Thus, without sun, there would be no life on the Earth.

Can you think of three other ways in which we use solar energy?

____

____

____

Plants Need Energy

You have already learned that green plants make their own food by **photosynthesis**. It is in the presence of sunlight that green plants make food using water and carbon dioxide. The food that plants make gives them the energy to grow and survive.

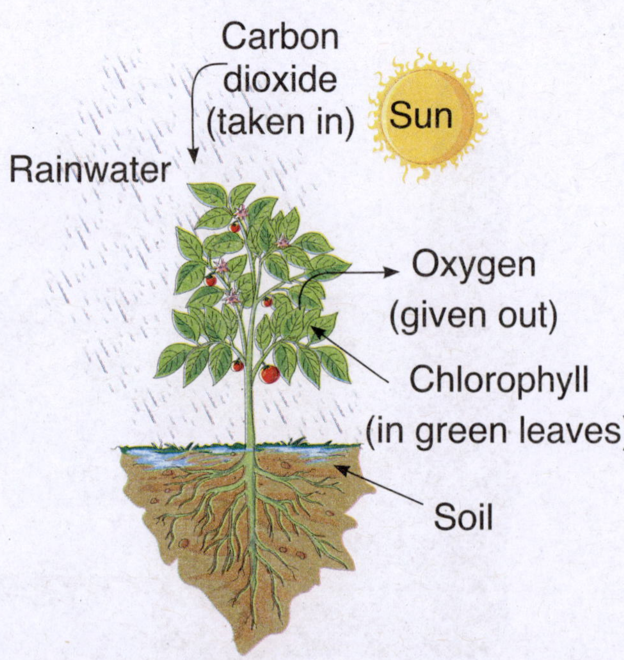

Plants use light energy from the sun to carry out photosynthesis.

How Do We Get Energy from the Sun?

A cheetah runs very fast. From where do you think it gets its energy to do so? Well, if your answer is food, then you are absolutely right. But from where do plants get the energy to make their food? The answer is the sun.

The picture below shows how energy from the sun is transferred to us.

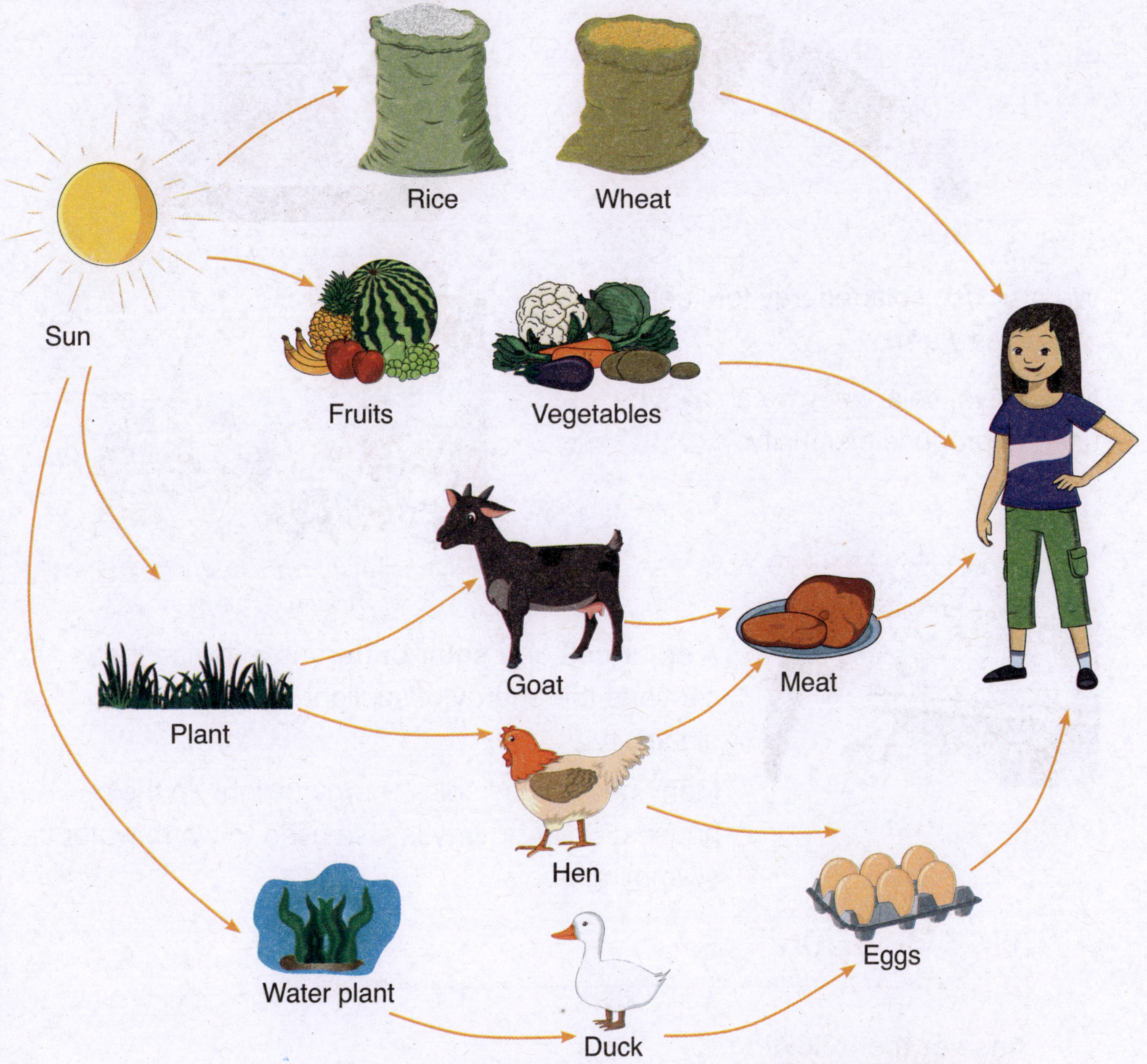

Transfer of energy from the sun to humans

Thus, we see that all the energy from plants and animals (through food) originally comes from the sun.

DO IT YOURSELF

Think of your favourite food. Can you trace the way it received its energy all the way from the sun? Draw and explain.

How Do We Use Solar Energy?

We use solar energy for drying clothes.

Clothes drying in the sun

Solar cookers convert sunlight to heat energy that is used for cooking or heating food.

Solar cooker

We also use solar energy for keeping ourselves warm.

Nowadays, solar energy can also be used to produce electricity.

Usage of solar energy for keeping ourselves warm

Solar energy harnessed through solar cells

A **solar cell** or a **solar battery** is a device that converts the energy of sunlight directly into electricity.

Many people use solar energy to light up their houses. Solar energy is also used to warm water in swimming pools.

QUICK REVISION

Answer the following.

1. Name the two forms of energy we get from the sun: ____________ and ____________
2. Name the process in which plants use light energy from the sun to make food: ____________
3. List any two uses of solar energy: ____________ and ____________

RENEWABLE AND NON-RENEWABLE SOURCES OF ENERGY

Renewable sources of energy are the resources that are **replenished** by the environment over a short period of time.

Water, wind and sun are all renewable sources of energy. Solar energy is a good source of renewable energy as the sun never stops shining.

WORD TO KNOW
replenished: replaced or refilled

Non-renewable sources of energy are the resources that have a limited supply and cannot be replaced easily once exhausted. Petrol, diesel and coal are examples of non-renewable sources of energy. We must be careful while using them as they cannot be replaced.

Wind energy harnessed through windmills

Conservation of Energy

It is important that we learn to save energy and conserve the non-renewable sources of energy. To conserve energy, we can do the following:

- Use a fan and not the air conditioner all the time.
- Switch off the lights and fans when you leave the room.
- Walk or cycle to a nearby place and avoid using a car as it saves fuel.
- Take short showers.
- Turn off all electrical devices when they are not in use.
- Use devices that run on solar energy, such as solar cookers and solar heaters, to save electricity.

FIND OUT What are fossil fuels?

A child riding a bicycle

Solar heater

CONCEPT MAP

Sun

- **Heat energy**
  - Keeps animals and human beings warm
  - Helps plants grow
  - Helps to produce electricity using solar panels
  - Helps to dry clothes
- **Light energy**
  - Helps plants make food
  - Helps us see things around us

KEYWORDS

Solar energy: energy obtained from the sun

Solar cell: a device that converts solar energy into electricity

Renewable sources of energy: resources that are replenished by the environment over a short period of time

Non-renewable sources of energy: resources that have a limited supply and cannot be replaced easily once exhausted

Exercise

Objective Type Questions

A. Choose the correct answer.

1. The energy that we get from the sun is called _______________ energy.
   a. lunar b. solar c. electric d. motor
2. The _______________ has no light of its own.
   a. star b. moon c. firefly d. electric torch
3. The main source of our energy is _______________.
   a. Sun b. food c. fuel d. air
4. A non-renewable source of energy is _______________.
   a. Sun b. wind c. petrol d. water
5. Solar energy is used to _______________.
   a. produce electricity b. to purify water
   c. to kill germs d. All of these

B. Write T for True and F for False.

1. The moon reflects the light of the sun.
2. Plants can make food only in the presence of sunlight.
3. Diesel is a renewable source of energy.
4. The sun is a non-renewable source of energy.
5. Some sources of energy have a limited supply.

C. Fill in the blanks.

1. Sunlight is needed by plants to make food by a process called _______________.
2. Solar energy is used to provide _______________.
3. Sunlight is a rich source of _______________.
4. We use solar energy for _______________ clothes.
5. A _______________ converts the sun's energy to electricity.

Subjective Type Questions

A. Answer the following questions in brief.

1. How does the light from the sun help us?
2. What is a solar cell?
3. Name two non-renewable sources of energy.
4. Why should we use non-renewable sources of energy carefully?
5. What is a solar cooker?

B. Answer the following questions in detail.

1. How do we use the energy from the sun?
2. How do plants use the energy from the sun?
3. Draw and explain how the energy from the sun is transferred to us through food.
4. How are renewable sources of energy different from non-renewable sources of energy?
5. Write any three ways you can conserve energy.

Application-based Questions

A. Why can't plants make food at night?

B. Why should we be out in the sun at least for some time in a day?

Picture-based Question

Tick the items that protect you from the strong sunrays.

Hat

Cotton clothes

Sunglasses

Woollen clothes

Sunscreen lotion

Skill Booster

A. 21CS: Creativity and Innovation | AI | BT: Psychomotor

Make your own solar cooker.

Materials needed: Shoebox with a lid that can be separated, aluminum foil, masking tape, ruler, scissors, black paper, ice cream stick and plastic wrap

1. Separate the shoebox and its lid.
2. Cover the inside of the box with aluminum foil. Use masking tape to secure the foil to the box.
3. Place the black paper at the bottom of the shoebox and on top of the foil.
4. Use your ruler to draw a rectangle on top of the lid, about 1 inch from the sides.
5. Cut along the three sides of the rectangle to create a flap (take care not to cut along the fourth side). Carefully fold back the flap.
6. Cover the inside of the flap with aluminum foil. Prop open the flap using tape and the ice cream stick.

7. Tightly stretch the plastic wrap over the opening in the lid and secure with tape.
8. Now, put some cheese between two salted biscuits and place it in the shoebox, and place the lid on top.
9. Now, place the box under the sun. Let the sunlight be reflected from the flap into the box. Check after fifteen minutes to see if the cheese has melted and your snack is ready.

B. **21CS:** Leadership and Responsibility | **AI** | **BT:** Psychomotor, Affective

In groups, make posters to show the different ways you can save energy. Put them up in different parts of your school to make everybody aware of the conservation of energy.

C. **21CS:** Critical Thinking | **BT:** Cognitive, Affective

One day, the Wind and the Sun had an argument. Each claimed to be stronger than the other. So, they agreed to have a test of their strength.

"I see a man travelling down the road. Let us see who takes off his scarf," said the Sun.

The Wind agreed and tried first. It blew very strongly. But the man wrapped his scarf even more closely around him.

Then came the Sun's turn. It shone gently at first. So, the man loosened his scarf. Then, the Sun started shining very brightly. The man started feeling hot and took off his scarf. The Wind had to accept its defeat.

What do you think is the moral of the story?

Worksheet 10

Tushar kept a plant in the balcony.

Disha kept a plant in her room.

My SEE Journal

A. After a month, what changes will Tushar see in his plant?

____

____

____

____

____

B. Compare the two plants after some days. Would you find any differences? Why?

____

____

____

____

____

My SDG Journal

15 LIFE ON LAND

A. How should Disha take care of her plant?

____

____

____

____

____

B. How is sunlight important for you?

____

____

____

____

____

11 Cleanliness, Health and Hygiene

Prior Knowledge

- Keeping our body and clothes clean
- Keeping our home, school and surrounding clean

Learning Objectives

- What keeps our body healthy
- Ways to improve our surroundings
- *Swachh Bharat Abhiyan*

LET'S GET STARTED

Look at the pictures given below. Are these children following good habits? Write Yes or No.

1 

Amit is inserting a pencil in his ear.

2 

Rehan is drawing on the walls of his room.

3 

Paramjeet is washing his hands before eating.

4 

Shilpa is throwing waste into a dustbin.

We all like to look good and feel good. To stay fit and healthy, we need to follow some habits.

PERSONAL CLEANLINESS

Keeping our body clean is an important part of staying healthy. It also helps us feel good about ourselves. Here are some good habits you should follow to keep yourself clean.

- Brush your teeth twice a day, in the morning and before going to bed.
- Scrub yourself clean with soap and water.
- Shampoo your hair regularly. Brush and clean it.
- Clip your nails regularly.
- Wash your hands before and after meals.

Brush your teeth twice a day.

Have a bath every day.

Looking After Our Body

We should look after our body to stay healthy and fit. Some ways to do this are given below.

Healthy Food

- Always eat freshly-cooked food.
- Avoid eating junk food every day. Eat healthy snacks.
- Drink at least eight glasses of water every day.
- Eat different varieties of fruits and vegetables daily.
- Avoid eating sweets and fried food daily.
- Always remember to keep the food covered.

Eat fresh and healthy food.

Drink plenty of water.

Clip your nails regularly.

Eat different varieties of fruits and vegetables.

Wash your hands before and after meals.

Wash your hair regularly.

Rest, Exercise and Recreational Activities

- We must go to bed early and rise early.
- Exercise and yoga keep us fit. Playing outdoor games not only keeps us active but the sunlight helps our body to produce vitamin D.
- A good posture while sitting and standing keeps our body fit and healthy.
  While sitting on a desk or table, our back should be straight and we should not **slouch** on the table. While standing, we should stand erect.

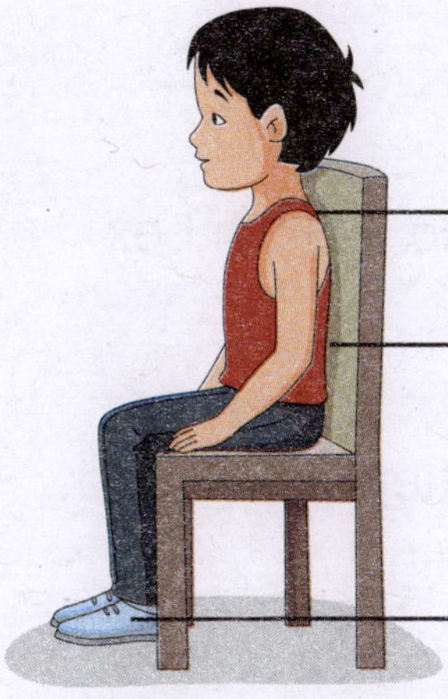

Sitting posture

DO YOU KNOW?

Our body makes vitamin D with the help of sunlight. Deficiency of vitamin D makes our bones weak.

WORDS TO KNOW

recreation: something that we like to do in our free time

slouch: to stand or sit lazily with your shoulders bent

Standing posture

Walking posture

- It is important to relax with friends and family. Going on a picnic to museums, parks and gardens, zoo, circus, theatre, musical programmes, films, etc., are some recreational activities that we enjoy.

QUICK REVISION

A. Circle the things that keep you clean.

pencil soap eraser toothbrush crayon comb lunch box

B. Write T for True and F for False.

1. We should brush our teeth only once a day.
2. We should always wash our hands before and after eating food.
3. We do not need to exercise and play to stay healthy.
4. We should sit and walk with our back straight.
5. It is important to relax and spend time with friends and family.

KEEPING THE SURROUNDINGS CLEAN

To stay fit and healthy, it is important to keep our surroundings clean. Dirty and unhealthy surroundings spread diseases.

Do not spit in the open.

Say no to plastic.

Some ways to keep the surrounding clean are as follows.

- Always throw garbage in bins. Use bins of different colours to separate wastes—those that decay (fruit and vegetable peels, paper, etc.) and those that do not decay (plastic and glass items).
- Do not litter.
- Avoid using plastic bags as much as possible.
- Spitting around is unhygienic and spreads diseases. Never spit in the open.
- Do not use the roadside as a toilet.
- Grow plants to keep your surroundings green.

GREENATHON

Adopt a plant!

Adopt a small plant in or around your school or home. Water it, add manure to it and observe it bloom and grow!

Use different coloured bins to separate wastes.

Children planting a tree

Swachh Bharat Abhiyan (Clean India Mission)

What is the meaning of the word *'swachh'*? Discuss with your friends.

How can you keep your surroundings *swachh*? Discuss.

Swachh Bharat Abhiyan (Clean India Mission) was launched by the Government of India on the occasion of Gandhi Jayanti on 2 October 2014. Gandhiji believed that "cleanliness is next to godliness".

The *Swachh Bharat Abhiyan* has the following goals.

- Promote cleanliness and hygiene in the villages and cities.
- Build public and household toilets.

- Make arrangements for proper disposal of waste and garbage.
- Provide clean and safe drinking water.
- Spread the message of good health.

TALK TIME

How do you keep your house clean?

Who all help to keep your house clean?

Where do you throw the garbage of your house?

Is the area around your house clean?

Swachh Bharat: Swachh Vidyalaya (school)

- All schools should have separate toilets for boys and girls.
- Washing hands with soap before and after eating and after using the washroom should be made a habit.
- Safe drinking water for children should be provided.
- Water for hand wash, school cleaning, food preparation and cooking should be sufficiently provided.
- Safe storage of drinking water should be available.

FIND OUT

Different coloured bins are used to collect different types of garbage.

Find out what each colour signifies.

CONCEPT MAP

Cleanliness

- **Personal cleanliness**
  - Brushing teeth
  - Taking a bath
  - Washing hair
  - Clipping nails
  - Washing hands after using the toilet
  - Washing hands before and after meals
- **Cleanliness of surroundings**
  - Throwing waste in bins
  - Avoiding plastic bags
  - Not using roadside as toilet
  - Using bins of different colours
  - Planting trees

Swachh Bharat Abhiyan

- Cleanliness in villages and cities
- Building public and household toilets
- Proper disposal of wastes
- Spreading the message of good health
- Safe and clean drinking water

KEYWORDS

Garbage: waste materials

Hygiene: cleanliness or maintaining good health through cleanliness

***Swachh Bharat Abhiyan*:** Clean India Mission

Exercise

Objective Type Questions

A. Choose the correct answer.

1. We get vitamin D from ______________.

   a. air b. sunlight c. water d. soil

2. We should avoid using ______________ bags.

   a. cloth b. paper c. plastic d. jute

3. We must separate garbage in bins of ______________ colour(s).

   a. same b. different c. only two d. only one

B. Write T for True and F for False.

1. We must brush our teeth only in the morning.
2. The sun helps our body to make vitamin C.
3. Watching a circus is a recreational activity.
4. *Swachh Bharat Abhiyan* was launched on the occasion of Republic Day.

C. Fill in the blanks.

1. We must drink ______________ glasses of water everyday. (two/eight)
2. Healthy food, exercise and ______________ keep us healthy. (activity/rest)
3. *Swachh Bharat Abhiyan* was started in ______________. (2011/2014)
4. We must maintain good ______________ while standing or sitting. (posture/hygiene)

Subjective Type Questions

A. Answer the following questions in brief.

1. Why should we play outdoor games?
2. Write two ways in which you can relax with your friends and family.

B. Answer the following questions in detail.

1. Write five ways in which we can keep ourselves clean.
2. What kind of food keeps us healthy?
3. List four ways in which we can keep our surroundings clean.
4. Describe a good posture.
5. What is the goal of *Swachh Bharat Abhiyan*?

Application-based Question

We should not use plastic bags in our daily lives. Why?

Picture-based Question

Separate the following garbage items in the right bins.

a torn book
a frisbee
a fused bulb
an old doll
an envelope
a broken mirror

Skill Booster

A. **21CS:** Creativity and Innovation | **AI** | **BT:** Psychomotor

Make your own Gift Wrapper!

Take two sheets of old newspaper. Paste the sheets together. Now, take a paint brush and paint designs on the paper. Let it dry. Roll and put away. Use when required.

B. **21CS:** Collaboration, Leadership and Responsibility | **EL** | **BT:** Psychomotor, Affective

Be a Litter Bug!

1. Make a litter squad. Go around your school. Pick up litter, if any, and put it in the bin.
2. Make posters (in groups) mentioning the different ways you can keep your school litter-free!

C. **21CS:** Information Literacy | **CC:** English | **BT:** Cognitive

Find five words related to cleanliness, health and hygiene in the given wordsearch.

T	O	O	T	H	P	A	S	T	E
X	H	W	A	S	H	I	N	G	K
U	S	Q	G	T	R	G	L	X	X
R	E	C	R	E	A	T	I	O	N
N	U	K	E	R	U	T	S	O	P
S	H	A	M	P	O	O	V	N	X
G	R	E	S	T	V	A	N	O	V
R	J	W	B	A	T	H	I	N	G
E	X	E	R	C	I	S	E	E	K
N	A	I	L	C	U	T	T	E	R

Worksheet 11

My SEE Journal

A. Why did the children call the picnickers selfish?

____

____

____

____

____

B. Why did the children think that the picnickers did not care about the Earth?

____

____

____

____

____

My SDG Journal

15 LIFE ON LAND

A. What arrangements should be there at picnic spots to keep the place clean?

____

____

____

____

B. How would you leave a picnic spot?

____

____

____

____

____

Review Corner

Review 1 (Chapters 1–3) **Maximum Marks: 25**

A. Fill in the blanks. **(4)**

1. Our body is made up of tiny units called ____________.
2. Plants breathe through tiny pores called ____________.
3. Earthworms breathe through their ____________.
4. Many organs together form a ____________.

B. Write the differences between the following. **(4)**

1. Exhaled air and inhaled air
2. Down feathers and flight feathers

C. The organs are mixed up. Put them back in their systems. **(4)**

kidneys skull nerves windpipe skin bones brain lungs spinal cord

Excretory	
Breathing	
Skeletal	
Nervous	

D. Choose the correct answer. **(2)**

1. ____________ is the part of the circulatory system.
   a. Lung b. Heart c. Kidney
2. ____________ is the place where two bones meet.
   a. Muscles b. Joint c. Skin
3. ____________ is a flightless bird.
   a. Dodo b. Emu c. Owl
4. ____________ protects the lungs.
   a. Ribcage b. Heart c. Brain

E. Answer the following questions. (Any two) **(6)**

1. What helps a bird fly?
2. What are the functions of the skeletal system?
3. What are the features of living things?

F. Label the parts of the digestive system given below. **(3)**

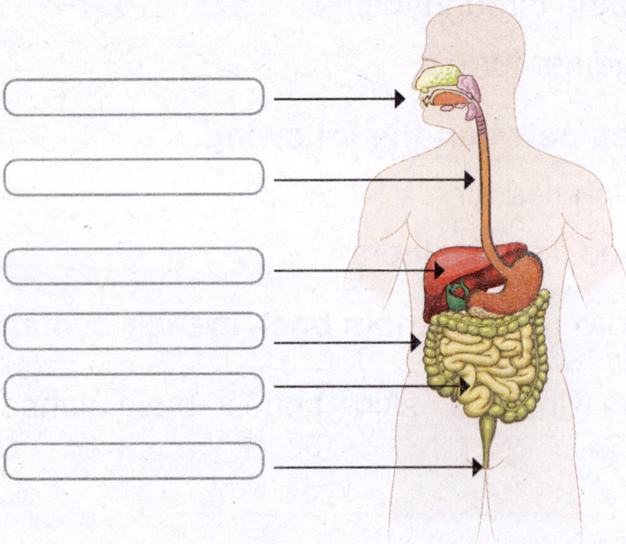

G. Mention one feature of the beaks of the following birds. **(2)**

1.  ____________

2.  ____________

3.  ____________

4.  ____________

Review 2 (Chapters 4–7) — Maximum Marks: 25

A. Fill in the blanks. **(4)**

1. Insects have ____________ to sense things around them.
2. A hard case called ____________ covers the pupa.
3. When a liquid changes into a gas, the process is called ____________.
4. ____________ have small, green and weak stems.

B. Choose the correct answer. **(2)**

1. ____________ does not suck blood.
   a. Leech b. Mosquito c. Butterfly
2. ____________ is a stem.
   a. Carrot b. Potato c. Radish
3. ____________ is the green-colouring substance in leaves.
   a. Stomata b. Chlorophyll c. Bud
4. ____________ is anything that has weight and occupies space.
   a. Mass b. Matter c. Evaporation

C. Write the differences between the following. (Any two) **(4)**

1. Social insects and harmful insects
2. Taproot and fibrous roots
3. A climber and a creeper

D. Answer the following questions. (Any three) **(9)**

1. Write three ways in which we can protect ourselves from diseases spread by insects.
2. Describe the three states of matter with examples.
3. List three functions of the root.
4. What are the functions of a leaf?

E. Label the body parts of the insect shown below. **(2)**

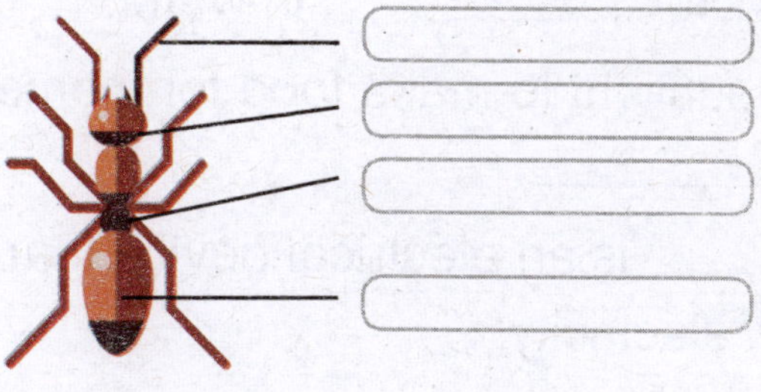

F. Draw and label the structure of a seed. Point out the seed coat, embryo, hilum and cotyledon in the structure. **(4)**

OR

Draw a leaf and label its parts.

Review 3 (Chapters 8–11) Maximum Marks: 25

A. Fill in the blanks. **(4)**

1. The changing of water vapour into water is called __________.
2. Boiling kills the __________ in water.
3. Plants use sunlight to make food for themselves through a process called __________.
4. A __________ is an electrical device that converts light energy directly into electricity.

B. Give reasons for the following. **(2)**

1. A good posture is important.
2. We must be careful while using non-renewable sources of energy.

C. Label the water cycle shown below. **(2)**

Water cycle

D. Choose the correct answer. **(2)**

1. When a solid changes into a liquid on heating, the process is called __________.

   a. freezing b. melting c. evaporation

2. We should clip our nails __________.

   a. everyday b. every week c. every month

3. Example of a renewable source of energy is __________.

   a. petrol b. coal c. water

4. __________ is not a source of water.

   a. Glacier b. Well c. Lime

E. Answer the following questions. (Any three) **(9)**

1. Write three physical properties of water.
2. What are the different methods of separating insoluble impurities from water. Describe any one method.
3. Write a short note on rainwater harvesting,
4. Write three ways in which we use solar energy.

F. Put a tick mark on the images that show good habit and a cross mark on those that show bad habit. **(2)**

1. 

2. 

3. 

4. 

G. Draw to show how solar energy is transferred to our body. **(2)**

H. Complete the crossword. **(2)**

Across

3. The purest form of water
4. The wastes

Down

1. Another word for water vapour
2. When a liquid changes into a solid

ENRICHMENT ZONE : Solar System, Moon and Stars

Prior Knowledge

- Sun in the sky during the day
- Moon and stars in the sky at night
- Twinkling of stars in the sky at night

Learning Objectives

- Solar system
- Names of the planets
- Phases of the moon
- Constellations

LET'S GET STARTED

Look at the pictures given below. Write any two differences between them.

1 

2 

1. ____________________

2. ____________________

In the daytime, we see the sun in the sky, and at night, we see the moon and the stars. In previous classes, you have learned about the sun, the moon and the stars. Let us learn more about them.

THE SOLAR SYSTEM

The sun and its family of eight planets together form the solar system.

DO YOU KNOW?

An *astronomer* is a person who studies heavenly bodies such as the sun, moon and stars.

The Sun

The sun is a huge ball of hot gases. It is actually a star. There are many stars in space, but the sun is the closest star to the Earth. That is why it looks so big.

Follow this mnemonic to remember the names of the planets!

My	-	Mercury
Very	-	Venus
Efficient	-	Earth
Mother	-	Mars
Just	-	Jupiter
Served	-	Saturn
Us	-	Uranus
Noodles	-	Neptune

Planets

A planet is a large, round object in space that moves around the sun. The eight planets of the solar system are Mercury, Venus, Earth, Mars, Jupiter, Saturn, Uranus and Neptune.

Planets move around the sun in fixed paths called **orbits**.

Jupiter is the largest planet, while Mercury is the smallest planet. Venus is the brightest planet in the solar system.

Mars is also known as the red planet due to its reddish appearance. Saturn is known for the beautiful rings around it.

Solar system (not to scale)

Earth

Earth is the third planet of the solar system. It is the planet we live on.

Life

Earth is the only planet known to have life on it. It has land, air and water, which are essential for life. Earth obtains heat and light from the sun. The sun is the source of all energy on the Earth.

DO YOU KNOW?

Though the sun is about 150 million kilometres away from the Earth, it takes only eight minutes for the sunlight to reach us!

Shape

The Earth is round in shape. It appears flat to us because we see only a small part of it. People who have travelled in space have taken pictures of the Earth, which clearly show that its shape is round.

Rotation of Earth

Movements

The Earth shows two types of movements. It spins like a top on an imaginary line called **axis** that passes through the centre of the Earth. This spinning movement is called **rotation**. It takes about 24 hours to complete one spin or rotation. The rotation of Earth causes day and night.

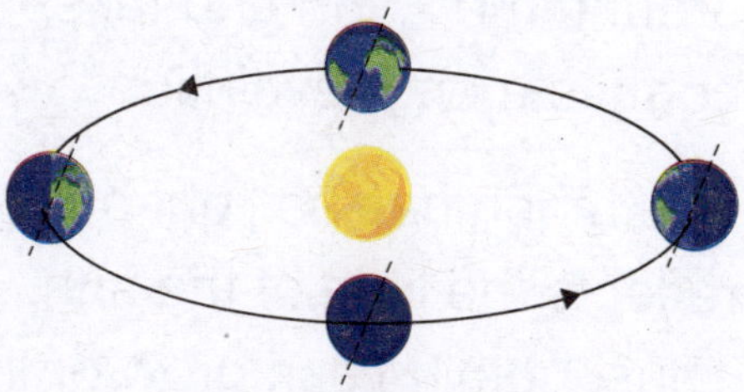

Revolution of Earth

The Earth also revolves around the sun in an imaginary path, that is, its **orbit**. This movement is called **revolution**. The Earth takes 365 days, 5 hours, 59 minutes and 16 seconds to complete one revolution. The revolution of Earth causes changes in seasons.

QUICK REVISION

Fill in the blanks.

1. The sun and the eight planets together form the ____________.
2. Planets move around the sun in fixed paths called ____________.
3. ____________ is the only known planet with life on it.
4. The spinning movement of the Earth on its axis is called ____________.
5. The ____________ of the Earth causes changes in seasons.

DO IT YOURSELF

1. Keep a globe on a table in a dark room.
2. Now, keep a table lamp in front of the globe.
3. When you switch on the lamp, you will see that the portion of the globe facing the lamp is lit up and the portion opposite to it is dark.

4. Mark a place on the bright side of the globe.
5. Now, slowly rotate the globe. You will see that the place you marked will be in dark after sometime.

This shows that the rotation of Earth on its axis causes day and night.

MOON

The moon is the Earth's closest neighbour. It is a natural satellite of the Earth. A **satellite** is an object that goes around a planet. The moon goes around the Earth and takes about 28 days to complete one revolution.

In 2014, Indian astronomers launched a satellite in the orbit of Mars. Find out its name.

FIND OUT

The moon has no light of its own. It shines because it reflects the light of the sun. The moon has no air or water. Thus, nothing can grow or live on the moon.

Looking through a telescope

The **telescope** is an instrument that makes faraway objects appear closer. It helps in studying heavenly bodies such as the moon and the stars.

When seen through a telescope, large pits are seen on the surface of the moon. These pits are called **craters**. The moon also has mountains on its surface.

Phases of the Moon

If you look at the sky carefully at night, you will see that the shape of the moon appears different on different days. As the Earth changes its position, at times, we see a bigger portion of the moon lit up, while at times, we see a smaller portion of the moon lit up. When the lit-up part of the moon goes on increasing, we say the moon is **waxing** and when the lit-up part of the moon goes on decreasing, we say the moon is **waning**.

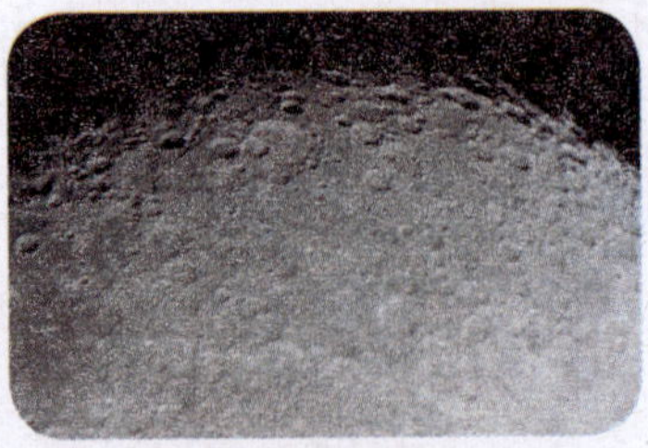

The moon seen through a telescope

The names given to the pattern of change in the moon's appearance are called the **phases of the moon**.

When the moon is between the sun and Earth, the side that faces the Earth does not get any sunlight; so we are not able to see the moon from Earth. This is the **new moon** or ***Amavasya***.

Then, after sometime, the moon starts increasing or waxing, and we are able to see half the moon. We call it **half moon**. Then, we see the entire moon when it reaches the opposite side of Earth. This is called the **full moon** or ***Purnima***. The transition from the New Moon phase to the Full Moon phase takes 14 days.

DO YOU KNOW?

Neil Armstrong was the first man to step on the moon in the year 1969.

After the Full Moon phase, the lit-up part of the moon starts decreasing or waning until it reaches the New Moon phase. This way, the cycle continues.

New Moon *Crescent Moon* *Half Moon* *Gibbous Moon* *Full Moon*

THE STARS

When you look at the sky at night, you see many stars twinkling. These stars have their own light and are made of hot gases. The sun is also a star.

When we look at the sky, it seems that some groups of stars form a pattern. These patterns are called **constellations**. Some well-known constellations are Great Bear, Gemini, Scorpio, Orion, Leo and Cancer.

The Pole Star or the North Star is the brightest star in the northern sky. In the olden days, travellers and sailors used to look at this star to find directions.

Orion *Great Bear* *Scorpio*

Exercise

Objective Type Questions

A. Underline the correct answers.

1. The solar system has (eight/nine) planets.
2. Mercury is the (smallest/largest) planet.
3. The moon is (an artificial/a natural) satellite of Earth.
4. The moon revolves around the (Earth/sun).
5. The Full Moon is called (*Amavasya*/*Purnima*).

B. Fill in the blanks.

1. A planet moves around the sun in a fixed path called the ____________ (axis/orbit).
2. Earth is the ____________ (second/third) planet from the sun.
3. Earth is ____________ (round/flat) in shape.
4. The instrument that helps us to see faraway things is called ____________ (microscope/telescope).
5. When the lit-up part of the moon increases, we call it ____________ (waxing/waning).

C. Write T for True and F for False.

1. Earth spins on its axis once in every 24 hours.
2. Earth is a star.
3. The moon has light of its own.
4. The Pole Star is the brightest star.

D. Name the following.

1. The dwarf planet ____________
2. The path followed by planets to move around the sun ____________
3. When the lit-up part of the moon goes on decreasing ____________
4. The brightest star in the northern sky ____________
5. Patterns made by groups of stars ____________

Subjective Type Questions

A. Answer the following questions in brief.

1. What is a satellite?
2. What is the position of the moon on a New Moon day?
3. What is a star made up of?
4. How did travellers and sailors find directions at night in the olden days?

B. Answer the following questions in detail.

1. How many planets are there in the solar system? Name them in order.
2. What is meant by the phases of the moon?
3. What are constellations? Can you name some constellations?

Application-based Questions

A. Why cannot we go to the moon for a holiday?

B. What do you think will happen if the Earth stops revolving?

Picture-based Question

Name the different phases of the moon.

1. ____________

2. ____________

3. ____________

4. ____________

5. ____________

Skill Booster

A. **21CS:** Creativity and Innovation, Information Literacy | **AI** | **BT:** Cognitive, Psychomotor

Make a chart of the solar system!

You will need: A black chart paper, balls of different types and sizes such as two ping pong balls, one cotton ball, two medium-sized balls, two large balls and one huge ball.

Method:

1. Paint the balls with the details of the planets. For example, a red ball for Mars, a green and blue one for Earth, etc. You can use the cotton ball for Mercury. Use the huge ball for Jupiter.
2. You can alternatively use different-coloured balls of varied sizes.
3. Make a sun and stick it at the centre of the chart paper.
4. Draw orbits to show the path of the planets around the sun and stick the balls to represent the planets in order and label them. Your solar system chart is ready!

B. **21CS:** Critical Thinking | **BT:** Cognitive

What do you think would happen if the Earth stopped rotating on its axis? How would it affect your life?

Happy Accidents

What Would You Like to Have for Breakfast?

Cornflakes are one of the most common choices for breakfast all around the world. It is a breakfast cereal made by toasting flakes of corn. Do you know how it was invented?

In the 1890s, two brothers, Dr John Harvey Kellogg and Will Keith, were experimenting with whole-grain dough to make thin rolled sheets of toasted crackers. One day, they left some cooked wheat for rolling unattended. When they got back, the cooled wheat was rolled out into thin sheets and baked in the oven. This turned out to be tasty and crispy and it paved the way for the cornflakes that we eat today. In 1898, they tried the same process using corn instead of wheat. In this way, "cornflakes" were born.

Do you know that cornflakes contain iron?

Let's find out!

NOTE Be safe: Keep strong magnets away from metal surfaces or electronics and keep magnets far apart and never put them together.

Things You Need

1. Cornflakes
2. A strong magnet
3. A zip-lock bag
4. Water

Let's Start:

1. 

   Put a cup of cornflakes into a zip-lock bag. Fill the bag halfway with water. Carefully seal the bag. Press the cornflakes with your fingers for a few minutes. Let the bag sit for about half an hour.

2. 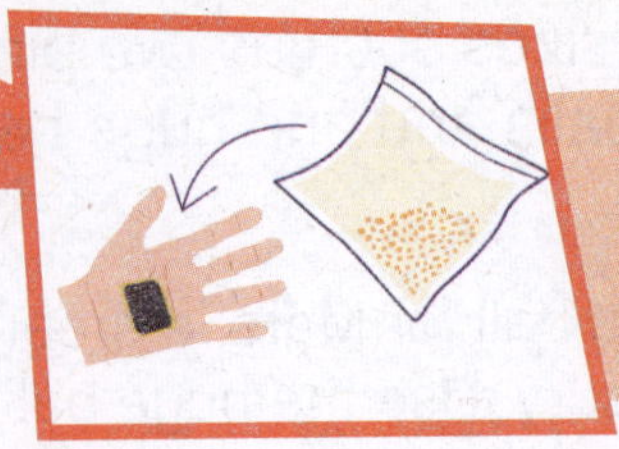

   Hold a magnet in your palm. Place the bag over the magnet.

3. 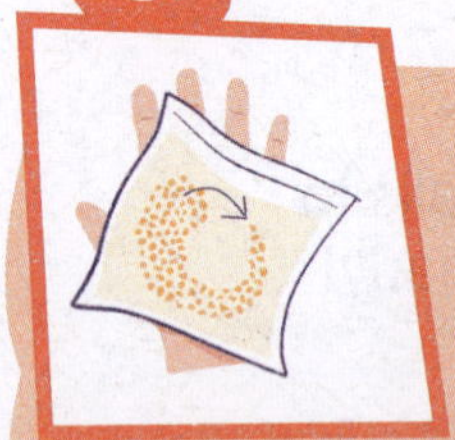

   Slowly tap the cornflakes inside the bag with the other hand for about a minute.

4. 

   Flip the bag and magnet together.

5. 

   Squeeze the mixture on one side and slowly move the magnet on the other side. Carefully look inside the bag around the edges of the magnet. What do you see?

Your Task

The sandwich that is so widely eaten also has an interesting history. Find out the details about the beginning of this remarkable yet versatile food item. Write a short note based on your findings.

A sandwich can be considered both a junk food and a healthy snack based on the items used in its preparation. Make a healthy sandwich and write the steps to make it. List out all the items that you will use in your sandwich. Write about how each item makes your sandwich healthy.

Innovation: The Steppingstone

A Portable Mobile Phone Holder

Chiraag's granny faced a serious issue. Her mobile phone's charging wire was quite short. She could not charge her phone without standing and holding her phone near the power point. She was finding it very difficult to charge her phone, standing and holding the phone near the power point.

Chiraag had a creative thought. He asked his mother to sew a small pouch with a loop. He gave the pouch to his granny. Nowadays, his granny charges her phone by putting the phone in the pouch and hanging it near the power point.

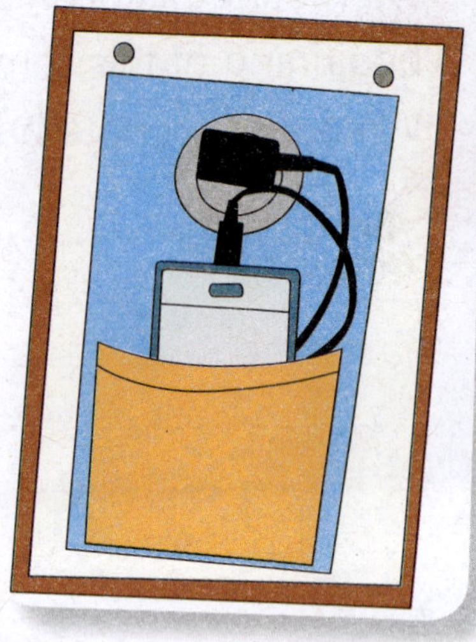

Like Chiraag, have you ever solved a problem? What was the problem and how did you solve it?

____

____

____

____

____

____

Draw or paste a picture of your innovation.